257

THE NATURE AND LIMITS OF
POLITICAL SCIENCE

THE NATURE AND
LIMITS OF
POLITICAL SCIENCE

BY

MAURICE COWLING

Fellow of Jesus College
Cambridge

CAMBRIDGE
AT THE UNIVERSITY PRESS
1963

PUBLISHED BY
THE SYNDICS OF THE CAMBRIDGE UNIVERSITY PRESS

Bentley House, 200 Euston Road, London, N.W.1
American Branch: 32 East 57th Street, New York 22, N.Y.
West African Office: P.O. Box 33, Ibadan, Nigeria

©

CAMBRIDGE UNIVERSITY PRESS
1963

Printed in Great Britain by
Spottiswoode, Ballantyne & Co. Ltd.
London and Colchester

PREFACE

The middle of this book contains comments on quotations from the work of a large number of scholars. Choice of quotation has been largely indifferent—so long as the quotation makes the point under discussion, so long as the work was published before the middle of 1961 and so long (generally) as the author is alive, or influential, in England. Many other scholars could have been chosen: and many other examples. The use of the word *rational* in the writings of Professor Ginsberg and Professor Greaves, for instance, would repay attention: though little would emerge that has not emerged from studying the use to which Professor Hart and Mr Peters put it also.

Since this is not intended as an historical work, no attempt has been made to give a comprehensive view of the work of any particular scholar. Inevitably, in these circumstances some scholars may be made to seem more foolish than they are. It cannot, therefore, too often be repeated that the quotations have one object—and one object only—to pinpoint by example ways of writing which those who offer political explanation should feel an obligation to avoid.

The author owes a large debt to Miss J. Fosbrooke-Ream of Wisbech and Cambridge for typing the book, to Mr J. A. Tuck for very kindly reading the proofs, to Professor Oakeshott and Mr Kedourie for commenting on the manuscript and to the Staff of the University Press for publishing it. He is grateful, also, to the Master and Fellows of Jesus College and the Master and Fellows of Peterhouse, both corporately and individually, for various sorts of sustenance during the period of composition.

He would like finally to thank all those who, at

various stages and in various places, have helped him to understand what political activity is like and what academic activity is for. They are, fortunately, so many that to thank all would be tedious. He wishes, however, to record the debt he has owed over the years to five teachers—to Raymond Clarke, the Reverend Charles Smyth, Charles Wilson, Professor Butterfield and Professor Michael Oakeshott. Though responsible for much, they are, needless to say, not responsible for what follows.

Jesus College,   MAURICE COWLING
Cambridge
1962

As the Christians (somewhat ungenerously) put it, the best approach to truth is through a study of error.

C. N. COCHRANE *Christianity and Classical Culture* (1939), p. vii

Philosophy, . . . rightly employed, will teach a lesson of humility to its disciple; exhibiting, as it does, the spectacle of a creature of finite intuitions, surrounded by partial indications of the Unlimited: of finite conceptions, in the midst of partial manifestations of the Incomprehensible.

H. L. MANSEL *The Limits of Religious Thought Examined* (1859), p. 66

By Liberalism I mean . . . the exercise of thought upon matters, in which from the constitution of the human mind, thought cannot be brought to any successful issue and is therefore out of place.

J. H. NEWMAN *History of my Religious Opinions* (1865), p. 288.

I

THIS IS an academic book. It is, however, meant to be academic and the author makes no apology for that. It is designed to suggest ways in which political studies can be rescued from the confusion into which they have fallen in England in the last sixty years and to indicate the turns they should take if the gains which have been made in the last ten years are to be extended into the future. In a negative direction, it stresses the truth (which arrogance masquerading as altruism and dogmatic certainty disguised as open-mindedness have in too many places obscured too long) that an essential preliminary to serious political explanation is to abandon the belief that those who write but do not rule would be rather better at ruling (if they had the chance) than those who do. When the direction of their interests is wrong academic subjects easily suffer periods of sterility. Sterility is not an invariable consequence of false assumptions; but the sterility of much contemporary academic political writing is.

An academic subject-matter arises when a world of activity is isolated from the whole of activity: when attempts are made to understand and explain it: and when its exponents obey the injunction to turn back upon the temptation to alter, control or participate in it. To turn back in this way is the beginning of explanatory activity, is the academic function: and the academic function is lost in irrelevance or practice if the injunction is ignored. Nothing in this respect distinguishes subjects commonly called scientific from those that are not. To control nature (except for the purpose of verifying hypotheses about its character) is as irrelevant to the academic concern as the attempt to impose on moral and political practice the ends enunciated by philosophers. The use to which Rutherford's (or Keynes's) work could be put in creating weapons of destruction or controlling unemployment has no relevance to the scientific concern—which ends when explanations can be verified so as to show that they seem, when judged by the relevant standard, right. Fertility and coherence, intelligibility and plausibility are the criteria by which explanation must be judged: and if one may properly speak of *political* science at all, it is only in the sense in which historians as well as chemists, philosophers as well as physicists are practitioners of sciences—in the sense in which, by providing bodies of explanation of the areas in which they work, they extend the range of understanding of the civilization of which they are a part. Authority in these matters is confined to explanation of the subject-matter: anything that scholars do beyond, they do, as it were, for profit or relaxation.

This is not to say that explanatory writers can never have practical authority, that moral decisions do not arise in connection with scientific explanation or that the moral implications of action are separable from the professional. Nor is it to suggest that faculties ought never to be set up, or universities established, in order to fulfil needs which those who exercise power or command wealth in any particular society have judged to be necessary. Most universities were founded in response to decisions of this sort—to maintain a religion, support a régime or increase the stock of medical, legal or scientific skill—and it would be the absurdest clerical conceit to suggest that they should not have been. Political authority, however, will be attributed to political writing so far as those who engage in practical activity are willing to give it. Academic authority will be attributed so far as its account of the character of political activity is intelligible, and the only activity to which an academic body, once established, should be committed is the activity of explanation. Anyone who wants in these circumstances to confine university disciplines within an academic framework will find much that passes for academic political science not only academically inadmissible, but also sterile and pretentious because, whilst affecting an academic manner, it performs the function (but wants the authority) of those who engage in political practice.

Little, therefore, is said in these pages about liberal democracy, the democratic ideal, social-democratic principles or the Welfare State and nothing whatever about Western values, the Two Cultures, the crisis of civilization, or Reconciliation (of religion to science, black to white or rich to poor). Nor is it asked whether Britain is a Good, Great or Open Society or whether she is an Affluent, Acquisitive or Irresponsible one. The political slogans of improving liberalism have no place in a work of this sort. 'Christianity', wrote Archdeacon Cunningham in 1908, 'has nothing whatever to do with modern social ideals.'[1] And nor, one may add, has political philosophy either.

Much is said, on the other hand, about the study of political subjects in English universities: and not without reason. It is in university departments of political science that much of the writing affecting the name goes on and universities, paradoxically enough, which maintain conditions productive of the major error on which the so-called science depends—a sense of shame at being academic, a fear that to be academic is less responsible

[1] W. Cunningham, *The Cure of Souls* (1908), p. 169.

3

than to have an influence on a world of practice wider than that involved in thinking coherently, writing books, teaching undergraduates and maintaining the integrity of an explanatory subject-matter.

Universities, in order to defend the academic function, have sometimes to engage in political action. This may be what Professor Beloff meant when he wrote that 'if the universities can give no guidance as to the methods by which the "problems [of] the modern world" can be solved, that advice will be sought elsewhere, *and to our disadvantage*'.[1] If this *is* what he meant, however, is it reasonable to add that 'Nuffield College represents part of the university's contribution to handling the problems of the modern welfare state: whereas St Anthony's helps us to tackle those that arise from the growing inter-dependence of the nations of Europe and beyond'?[2] It may be that government is sometimes helped by work produced within these walls, some of which is of high academic quality. But would it so obviously work to the university's, or country's, disadvantage if these two foundations had not been dedicated to the Social Sciences, or if, instead of studying *The British General Election of 1959* or *The Far East in World Politics*, Mr Butler and Mr Geoffrey Hudson had turned their considerable energies *Towards a text of Cicero: Ad Atticum* or the English Revolution of 1688?

Nor is political commitment without its dangers. Mr Gunnar Myrdal[3] justifies his desire to see social scientists play a part in public discussion of contemporary crises by claiming that, 'when addressing themselves to the public, the social scientists have always appealed . . . against social superstitions . . . in people's points of view . . . to the people's rationality' and, in doing so, 'have

[1] M. Beloff, *The Tasks of Government*, Inaugural Lecture, Oxford 1958, p. 7.
[2] Beloff, p. 8.
[3] G. Myrdal, *Value in Social Theory* (1958).

4

carried on the most glorious tradition of the Enlightenment'.[1] He claims that 'in these present catastrophic . . . circumstances [in international relations] what is urgently needed is a free, full, frank, calm and penetrating discussion on the highest intellectual level of the diverse causes of international tension . . .' conducted by 'independent scholars who can afford the freedom of detachment, serenity and courage'; and he concludes that Mr Walter Lippmann (whose freedom to comment is said to have been hampered by the Cold War) would, 'like Kennan, be very welcome among the professors'. One may wonder whether the *causes* of tension are now or were in 1953 (when Mr Myrdal wrote) in doubt, and, if they are, whether adequate explanation of their origin would make it easier to resolve them in practice. One may remark further that, although Mr Lippmann might have been 'welcome' among the professors, it is reasonable to hope that he would find a place only if his work amounts to as adequate an explanation of the nature of political activity as Mr Kennan's does of those segments of the past to which he has devoted attention. Universities have no obligation to provide pulpits for enlightened publicists: and if they do accept the obligation, thay may have to take the consequences. If 'it is', as Mr Myrdal remarks, 'a most unfortunate and potentially enormously dangerous effect of the cold war on the Western societies—most apparent in America, least in Britain—that even academic discussion now tends to be hampered by anxious forethought and fixed in opportunist stereotypes', then the situation is regrettable. 'Loyalty to provoked popular prejudice or the transient policies of the government of a state was', as he observes, 'never the signum of a science.'[2] But opposition to them is not the signum of a science either: and if those who are respon-

---

[1] Myrdal, p. 19.   [2] Myrdal, p. 25.

sible for academic explanation maintain the pretension to superior political rationality maintained by Mr Myrdal, they cannot reasonably expect to avoid the difficulties encountered by anyone who tries to exercise political power. If scholars insist on trying to exercise direct political power, they should not be surprised if their explanatory activity is curtailed as a consequence. In societies where the instability of government or prevailing political conventions make all political criticism dangerous, this will often be unavoidable. Explanation of the subject-matter is a scholar's only professional concern, and if attempts to *explain* contemporary practice produce restrictions on academic freedom, then a university will come into conflict with government. There is, however, only the thinnest line between explanation with a view to further explanation and explanation with a view to political action. Academic bodies are right to resist assaults on the first but have no reason to be concerned about the second. If, when they do, their freedom is restricted, or if (in immediately English terms) a party political factor came to affect the distribution of Government aid to universities, then the remedy most likely to advance the academic function would sometimes be curtailment of political commitment rather than the further commitment which complaint and protest would involve. 'Academic freedom' is a persuasive slogan. It is in practice, however, a complicated one: and only arrogance, naïveté, or serious misunderstanding could make Mr Myrdal claim that universities ought both to concern themselves with political practice and at the same time claim freedom from the uncertainty which political practice involves.

The view advanced here restricts the academic function, but that is what it is intended to do. Little is gained, and much is likely to be lost, by pretending that the academic function is more extensive than it is. The activities with which an academic subject ought to be concerned are neither necessarily connected with the teaching of undergraduates nor always best conducted by managers of pedagogic universities. Scholars who have never taught an undergraduate are capable of contributing to this sort of explanation. Many in the past have done so and there is no reason why others should not do so in the future. Nevertheless, prevailing interests in English universities make it probable that political studies, if they are to flourish in England in the immediate future, will flourish within (rather than outside) their walls. This is not necessarily a bar to intelligent political writing but, just as the academic political scientist may avoid temptations to which others might succumb, so they face temptations which others might avoid. The desire of some undergraduates for political indoctrination: the anxiety felt by the professional intelligentsia (often a scholar's own pupils) to present popular versions of his work in the organs of opinion over which they exercise control: the tendency (when so many organs of the higher journalism maintain a particular brand of practical liberalism) to offer for popular consumption practical commitment dressed up as philosophical reflection; and the danger that the scholar (on going into business as a prophet) will not only mistake his own political prejudices for philosophical reflection but will also produce reasons to justify his confusion—all these things may, in their various ways, prevent the academic political scientist pursuing the tasks to which he ought to be attending.

Something, therefore, is said in this volume about journalism and here there is a danger of misunderstanding. To the aggressive, prejudiced journalism of the large-circulation newspapers, the author has no objection of principle (though sometimes some of taste). Of newspapers, on the other hand, which affect impartiality and superior wisdom and presume to show by rational or disinterested consideration what all right-thinking men must obviously want, he has the greatest distrust. Journalism is a game which uses the public's wish to be informed or entertained in order to make money or influence opinion: so long as it pretends to nothing more, it is tolerable. But once the attempt to inform gives way to the pretension to preach, irrelevance begins. This is not less true if one source of influence is to affect a piety appropriate to religion. Nor is it irrelevant in considering an academic subject whose most important assumption is the belief—abandoned when excuses are made for new régimes in Asia or Africa but strong still in relation to those who exercise power at home—that power, when exercised without extensive public discussion, not only makes political science difficult but is also in an obvious sense irresponsible.

Much, finally, is said about religion: and again with good reason. Moral and political studies grew to independence in English universities in the shadow of assaults, sometimes in the name of science and enlightenment, sometimes in the name of historical criticism, on the dominance of theology, the truths of Christianity and its authority in moral practice. Studies emerged which professed to exercise over all right-thinking men the 'moral' and 'scientific' authority which Christianity had amongst Christians but which these studies were supposed to have greater authority to command. Assumptions, nevertheless, continued: presuppositions remained: and arbitrary certainties appropriate to religion were maintained by an intellectual interest which lacked a church, a special revelation or any particular God. A religion, however, without these conveniences is a religion nonetheless; its priests, secular by profession, high-minded by inclination and dissenting sometimes by manner and tradition, affected an authority in distributing moral and practical advice even more extensive than the religion they had abandoned. Philosophy in place of theology, morality in place of religion, political science instead of Christian duty seemed an impressive advance towards an ethically commanding sociology; whereas all that had happened was that one set of unarguable assumptions (supported by a Visible Church, an ecclesiastical establishment and an extensive educational system) had been replaced by another which did not escape a basis of arbitrary belief which its exponents supposed they had avoided.

The impact of this temper was profound. Erosion of the unselfconscious certainty of the truths of Christianity, which occurred to a significant degree amongst a significant part of the English intelligentsia between 1840 and 1900, was of the greatest consequence. Once an unselfconscious Christianity had become difficult, 'reasons' had to be given for what had previously been believed without 'reasons': and once 'reasons' become necessary, Christianity became merely one set of opinions with no more necessary authority than any other. The committed intelligence took liberty to pick and choose: religion was judged according to standards that now appeared more fundamental and it no longer seemed reasonable for anyone to believe anything without claiming to reconcile it with the beliefs of everyone else.

This tendency to judge and these standards of judgement are what we mean by Liberalism—not the slogans of a political party, not a body of economic doctrine and nothing to do with 'liberality of outlook', 'the liberal arts' or a 'liberal education'—but the extension of

9

conscientious theological doubt, which begins by demanding reasons for everything that is believed and ends by demanding reasons for everything that is done: which endangers by reference to interrogating principle not only the unargued certainties of religion but the unargued assumptions of action also: and which induces the illusion that men, because they are free to think, are free in each generation to lift themselves up by their bootstraps, to choose exactly what they ought to do and find rational moral principles and rational reasons for doing it. Optimism about consequences and the illusion of rational agreement about ends is the characteristic limitation of political thinking in this manner. It is, however, the manner in which a major part of the English intelligentsia, and most political scientists, have for long thought about politics: and even when theology has been reactionary or political content illiberal, Gore and Temple, Tawney and Scott Holland, Canon Demant and Lord Hailsham, have been not less guilty of subjecting political action to an unbearable weight of 'principle' because they avoid the pantheism, agnosticism and theological doubt characteristic of the positions we describe.

Those who want this sort of political science want something they cannot have. The assurance that prejudices are principles, preferences reasons, and the arbitrary opinions they adopt a rational expression of the universal law, is something political science cannot supply. But, if an ethically commanding science is an impossibility, an ethically indifferent philosophy is not. If political science in this sense is an illusion, political explanation, whose function is not to guide, exhort or preach, whose conclusions command to no particular line of action and whose object is simply to understand, is neither illegitimate nor undesirable.

This is political philosophy—the liquidator of normative sociology and political science, the outcome of the reflective intelligence discerning intelligibility in the world of practice: and it is to this (and to certain sorts of historical explanation) that attention ought now to be directed.

Philosophy here means metaphysics: and for this some apology may seem necessary. Metaphysics, so far from being superseded, as one sort of sympathetic apologetic suggests, by a religious command to see the world in a special way and live a special sort of life, should be seen as the outcome of reflection upon the fact that to see the world in a special way is no guarantee that a life can be lived that is consonant with it. The discontinuities apparent in human experience—between intention and consequence, ambition and accomplishment, knowledge of what it is right to do and capacity to do it—are not the result of verbal confusion, systematic error or incapacity to see the world for what it is (though a foolish metaphysic may make things seem more difficult than they are). They are on the contrary limitations embedded in all human situations which, though requiring in practice to be circumvented or ignored, in philosophy call for explanation with whatever tools a generation finds it helpful to employ. Some metaphysical systems, ignoring the discontinuity, imply that a particular sort of explanation commands to a particular sort of action: but there is no reason why they should. The characteristic of metaphysical explanation is not that it commands to action, but that it is intelligible and coherent and shows how far a philosopher's mind has grown by living through the difficulties under consideration. The intelligence, inventiveness and, where moral and political questions are concerned, the range of difficulties illuminated by Hobbes, Plato, Aristotle and Hegel are, whether one finds their accounts acceptable or not, considerable: and continued attempts to account for them will satisfy any legitimate ambitions political philosophers may have in future.

It is often said that political theory in England is dead and that the possibility of revival has been prevented by the rise of philosophical analysis. If, however, by political theory is meant (what Professor Cobban for example means[1])—provision of injunctions to 'rational' action—there is no reason to think it is. England shows, on the contrary, a vast persuasive literature whose purpose is to give reasons for adopting particular lines of political action and for attempting to establish a more 'sensible', more 'rational,' more 'enlightened' style of polity. Other squadrons exist: but the liberal, democratic, humanitarian one 'represents the most powerfully organized squadron in our [political] world at the present time'[2]: and it certainly provides the sort of guidance that Professor Cobban seems to want. Not all of it, of course, *looks* as though it is fulfilling the function that Green, Mill and Hobhouse or their eighteenth-century predecessors fulfilled. Bow Group and Fabian Society publications are obviously persuasions to action: and so are Mr Crosland's *The Future of Socialism*, Mr Raymond Williams's *The Long Revolution* and Dr Glanville Williams's *The Sanctity of Life and the Criminal Law*. Professor Beloff has not only produced two works, and a great deal of journalism which performs the practical function but also argues that political scientists have a responsibility to perform it. Mr Plamenatz's *On Alien Rule and Self-Government*, though in intention analytical, is in effect persuasive. Dr Kitson Clark's *The Kingdom of Free Men* is an eloquent persuasion

---

[1] Alfred Cobban, *In Search of Humanity* (1960), pts. I and IV.
[2] Cf. H. Butterfield, *George III and the Historians* (1957), p.10.

to liberal-conservative positions. Professor Brogan's *The Price of Revolution* is an abridged, synoptic and didactic evaluation of the good, and harm, done by the revolutionary movement in world history since 1776. Professor Butterfield (despite the uneasiness they might be expected to have caused the author of *The Whig Interpretation of History*) has, in the last thirteen years, produced four works which attempt to persuade to particular attitudes in political practice. Professor Jewkes and Lord Robbins amongst dons, Mr Christopher Hollis and Mr Schwarz amongst journalists have added to guidance. Penguin Books and Sir Charles Snow, the Brains Trust and Dr Bronowski have added to uplift. Professor Cobban shows signs of feeling a desire to resume the prophetic mantle he abandoned in 1943. And if some of these writers want a certain fashionable earnestness, others can supply that in abundance also.

There is, in fact, an extensive literature which gears general principles to political problems in order to suggest what various writers from various traditions think the political situation demands. Why, then, does Professor Cobban suppose that political theory is dead? Chiefly, it must be supposed, because he misunderstands the function performed by earlier political philosophers, attributes to the connections they made between their philosophical explanation of the nature of society and their practical injunctions greater necessity than they possessed, and because he wants his contemporaries to argue the 'philosophical' foundations of their principles. Green's injunctions do not follow necessarily from his explanation. That he supposed his philosophical position to have practical relevance does not alter the fact that others, from a similar explanation of the nature of moral rightness, drew different conclusions about its content. From almost any of Mill's 'principles' a

13

variety of practical programmes can be deduced: and almost all of Hobhouse's sociological explanations can be used to justify, not only the policies he desiderated but almost any other policies that could be desired. The practical injunctions contained in *On Liberty*, *Utilitarianism* and *Representative Government*, in Green's *Principles of Political Obligation* and in Hobhouse's *Principles of Social Justice* need not command greater practical authority because they were written by writers of high philosophical competence; nor does their philosophical competence diminish the arbitrary character of the injunctions. The status of the body of Victorian political reflection is, so far as guidance and advice are concerned, no different from that of the persuasion produced today (or then) in newspapers and magazines, on the television and in works by committed propagandists. Articulation of reasons is no necessary mark of authority in political practice: and the fact that reasons are articulated does not make a work a contribution to explanation either. Professor von Hayek, after describing 'that ideal of freedom which inspired modern Western civilization and whose partial realization made possible the achievements of that civilization',[1] asserts that since 'foreign policy today is largely a question of which political philosophy is to triumph over another . . . the lack of firm beliefs puts the West at a great disadvantage'. It is clear that he is concerned here about the consequences of this 'lack' in practice. It is clear also that, so far from undertaking the explanatory task, he is undertaking the practical one of finding for the 'West' a set of beliefs in order to restore its ability to 'use' the principles from which it is supposed to have grown. This, however, so far from being the task of the political philosopher, provides, on the contrary, material for his comment.

[1] F. von Hayek, *The Constitution of Liberty* (1960), p. 1.

The first comment to be made is that foreign policy is not 'largely a question of which political philosophy is to triumph'. And the second is that to speak as Professor von Hayek does[1] of 'civilization' being 'built' on 'basic principles' is a misleading abridgement. Commitment to 'principles' frees neither men nor societies from the accidents of historical development, and since, in these circumstances, Professor von Hayek's principles provide no comprehensive account of the growth of Western Europe, their status is attested, not by the 'history of western civilization', but by whatever persuasion his lucidity can effect in practice. Professor von Hayek in a sense recognizes this. 'This book', he writes,[2] 'is not concerned mainly with what science teaches us ... but to picture an ideal, to show how it can be achieved, and to explain what its realization would mean in practice.' One would, however, be happier with this disavowal of 'scientific' pretension if he did not add[3] that, so far from providing 'a detailed programme of policy', he prefers 'rather to state the criteria by which particular measures must be judged if they are to fit into a régime of freedom', that 'such a programme ... must grow out of the application of a common philosophy to the problems of the day', and that, on the way to approaching 'more tangible problems and as it proceeds', the book 'as a statement of general principles, must deal mainly with basic issues of political philosophy'.[4] Professor von Hayek's discussion of the meaning of *freedom* is powerful: his attempt to give it determinate content intelligent: but the only sense in which 'the basic issues of political philosophy' are dealt with in his volume is the unargued, and in the present writer's view indefensible, sense in which philosophy provides a guide to action. Writers

[1] von Hayek, p. 1. [2] von Hayek, p. vii.
[3] von Hayek, p. 5. [4] von Hayek, p. 5.

15

like Professor von Hayek, whatever Professor Cobban may think they are doing, perform the same function as Mill, and show that it is not practical political writing which is 'dead', but academic explanation itself. And if, instead of regretting the absence of a style of persuasive writing which exists in abundance, Professor Cobban had considered the condition of academic political science, his complaints would have had more substance.

The condition of explanatory political writing is, indeed, depressing. Contributions from academic writers in the last fifteen years have been thin and contributions from academic political scientists thinner. Amongst those who have been dominant in this period, certain names command respect—Professors Hart, Oakeshott and Mackinnon, Professors Popper, Emmett and Gluckman, the late Dr Weldon, Professor von Hayek and Sir Isaiah Berlin, Mr Mabbott and Mr Plamenatz, Professor Ginsberg and Dr Glanville Williams and a handful of others: but there is, apart from the substantial body of historical, legal and economic writing about which more will be said later, very little else of consequence. When Professor Beloff is not expressing political opinions or supporting political causes, he is almost always writing history. The body of Professor Brogan's work also is written in an historical manner and is, where contemporary subjects are concerned, so much the outpouring of a hard-headed, exuberant and sophisticated impressionist as to defy methodological limitation. Sir Ivor Jennings's *The Law and The Constitution* (published in 1933) was an admirable essay in political science: its quality has not been equalled since its author's interests have become more exclusively historical. Messrs Rees, MacIntyre, Wollheim, Williams and Watkins offer occasional hints at defining the subject-matter: and Mr Winch offers something a good deal more systematic. The writings of Messrs Benn and Peters (and Professor Greaves's *The Foundations of Political Theory*), are open to considerable methodological objection. Mr Kedourie, Mr Parkin, Dr Warrender and other historians of thought are writing, not political philosophy, but various sorts of historical explanation; while Mr Bernard Crick's *In Defence of Politics* (which appeared too late for detailed examination[1]) provides a convenient example of that illegitimate general reasoning against the academic claims of which the argument of the present book is directed. There is in addition an extensive body of writing which, under the names of political institutions, political sociology, comparative government, international relations and so on, might seem to provide political explanation; but which in general, as we shall see in a moment, is either defective history or so heavily impregnated with a practical purpose as to lack the academic dimension.

At a certain stage in the development of an academic subject, when the landmarks have disappeared from sight, attempts must be made to bring them back to view. It may be that explanatory political writing has in England always been rare but that is no reason why there should not be more of it in the future. In *political* philosophy, no more than in any other, are there definitive works and this is not a comprehensive work of political philosophy. If not this, however, it is offered as a destructive preliminary whose use will be justified by the conditions in which it is written. Philosophical analysis, whatever it has done elsewhere, has not in political studies confined the philosopher's attention to matters with which he is competent to deal: and, so long as ontological preoccupations are rejected, it is unlikely that it will. The position maintained here (and argued

---

[1] As did Professor J. D. B. Miller's *The Nature of Politics* (1962).

in the first half of the book) is that the landmarks of political science have long ceased to be noticed, academic principles ignored and ambiguity allowed to flourish. For the purposes of political practice, it matters very little whether ambiguity flourishes or not. But if the academic intention is to prevail where the academic subject-matter is concerned, certain confusions must be avoided in the future.

The first confusion arises from a tendency to forget that consequences are as important as intentions and that the consequences of even the most limited intentions are at the mercy of many factors over which no single will can have control. It is the oldest political cynicism in the world to observe that, once a slogan has served to bring a politician into office, political responsibility involves him in adopting policies which are different. To condemn politicians for this no doubt pleases those who observe, without participating in, the political struggle: but it would aid understanding greatly to recognize that the practice is so extensive as to constitute a normal political activity. Even when politicians put into practice the principles they proclaim, the intractibility of the political material often makes them draw back. Even when they do not willingly draw back, the progress of society deflects intentions, makes nonsense of principles and diverts purpose into directions which were never intended. And even when they convince themselves that they have achieved some large or generous revolution, the chief change which is often revealed, when the rhetoric has died away, is that a new group exercises power (or enjoys privileges) which another exercised (or enjoyed) before. Sometimes, no doubt, a change of person is the most important sort of revolution: but when, for example, 'nationalization of the means of production' turns out to mean that a new group of managers exercises power which colliery owners exercised before, one wonders whether the particular character of the change bears any relation to the heat of the language which was used in order to effect it. It is, moreover, not the case that good purposes are likely to have good consequences and bad purposes bad consequences or that, if those who set up as political teachers can induce men to act foolishly, they can induce them to act sensibly as well. There is no reason to believe that good men will be rewarded or bad ones punished or even that those whose purposes are presented in immaculate language are likely to succeed. Wherever one looks, one finds unexpected accident, unforeseen clash, unpredictable predicament breaking in upon the deliberate purposes of men: and the fact that this is so means that much more must in explanation (whatever may happen in action) be imputed to the movement of events than certain sorts of compulsive fussiness allow.

The second confusion arises from a tendency to forget that intentions are as important as consequences, and that, in explanation, it is difficult to determine the intention of any particular actor and misleading to infer it from the consequences of his action. The goodness of an action resides not in the consequences merely but in the intention also; and the connection between intention and consequence is as devious as the nature of the intention is elusive. A political decision may in its outcome have undesirable consequences: laws may have effects not intended by the legislator: but those who exercise power *have* intentions; make their decisions according to the standards they follow, and, even when the outcome does not turn out for the best, their intentions should not be taken any less seriously because events have not responded to them. Maximization of goodness (whatever its content) is the object of moral activity but success must be measured, not just by consideration of intention alone, but by reference to the part played by intention, by the act itself, and by its consequences in the whole history of the world. Consequences which are not intended play their part as much as those which are: and, if the outcome is favourable, must be judged to have moral worth. Professor Hart lists amongst his objections[1] to certain sorts of legal interference with sexual conduct, the fact that 'morality is valueless if enforced', and asks, 'what *moral* value is secured if people abstain from sexual intercourse simply out of fear of punishment?' But is the opportunity to act morally present only when the temptation to do otherwise is unhampered by legal pressure? Is there any reason to assume that the rightness or wrongness of an action must be determined by the free choice of the individual alone? No doubt, the possibility of choice and the opportunity to err increase the difficulty of doing right: but choices made out of fear of punishment rather than love of virtue can certainly produce consequences that are good. Not only does no man make all his choices for himself, but every man is also the embodiment of the moral conception of the society of which he is a part. Action may be good when an individual has, in a sense, 'chosen freely' but it is not, in order to be good, essential that he should have done.

Thirdly, there is a tendency to suppose that by studying 'the structure of contemporary government' light will be thrown on the way in which governments work—as though those who govern make public the factors which determine the decisions they take. Not only is it unlikely that their explanations will reveal their intentions: it is likely, on the contrary, that they will conceal them.

[1] H. L. A. Hart, *Oxford Lawyer* (Hilary, 1961), p. 8.

And not only in trivial or unimportant matters but in important matters also: and the more important the matter, the more likely is concealment to occur. English political conventions have never involved governments in making total revelation of the policies they pursue. Those who govern have had to take actions for which the reasons cannot be given: and often the reasons that are given are designed to lead those who study them as far away from the true reasons as possible. The speeches of politicans, the statements of ministers and the publications of government departments are designed not only to inform but also to persuade: unless they are studied in this light, they are unlikely to be understood. Unfortunately, contemporary political statements can seldom be studied in this way because the material which explains why they were made is missing, and the more recent the period studied, the more likely is this to be the case. It is difficult to believe that, for the purpose we have in mind, much illumination can come from studying any period before 1500 (when letters begin to be available in bulk) or after about 1920 (when, in England at least, essential ones cease to be available at all): and the more determined the effort to provide an education in contemporary politics by studying works like Mr Chapman's *The Profession of Government*, the Rector of Exeter's *Government by Committee*, Dr Robert McKenzie's *British Political Parties*, Mr Richards's *Honourable Members*, Mr David Butler's election studies or the body of writing which emerges from the shadows of Professor Robson and Titmuss at the London School of Economics and Professor W. J. M. Mackenzie at Manchester, the farther away from any understanding of the deviousness of all political activity are writers (and teachers) likely to be led.

The objection to this sort of history is that, since it

shows only the outside of *what* happened and not at all *how* it happened, it tends to imply that nothing else *could* have happened. This may be no bad thing in political practice (where reminder of the accidental character of established policies and the fragility of established reputations can be disturbing), but in explanation it is useless. Attempts to record the public appearance of events provide work that is useful to journalists. The public appearance of what happened is, for any purpose, important: but for intelligible explanation it is not enough. For every alternative policy adopted, four or five are rejected: and knowledge of these is as important as knowledge of the one. That Lord Home became Foreign Secretary in 1960 is an outward fact. What is not an outward fact, but what is of the greatest importance, is to know why *he* was appointed and no one else, and what process of calculation in the Prime Minister's mind, or manoeuvring on the part of others, brought him into office. It may be that he was appointed because he suited the Prime Minister's temperament. It may also be that this event, like many others, can be explained comprehensively by those who know—and more simply than the melodramas of political commentors imply. But, whatever the reality, the reality is difficult to explain if the central information is missing: and, until political scientists discover some means of finding it, their writings will lack a necessary dimension.

Power is exercised and decisions made, not by vast movements of opinion, but specifically by individual men: and there is in England, as much as anywhere in Western Europe, a tradition of reticence about the way in which they come to their conclusions. Sometimes those who conduct these studies show signs of recognizing that this is so. Mr David Butler admits that much

22

remains to be done, 'that there are still major political institutions and processes in Britain about which remarkably little has been recorded':[1] but neglects to draw the conclusion suitable to an academic discipline— that, since the basic material is not available, much of the subject is not worth pursuing at all. What do Mr Butler's works, and the works of his predecessors and collaborators, reveal about the intentions of the party managers at the five post-war elections? No doubt it is reasonable to assume that the object on each occasion (in the two major parties) was to win the election (though, even on so general a question, some *may* on some occasions have anticipated a victory so small that it would be better to plan for a greater victory later). It is doubtful whether officials of the great parties reveal very much more than they want to reveal: and it is impossible in present conditions to know what were Lord Woolton's electoral tactics in 1950 or 1951, or how far they succeeded. Yet, if this central facet of British electoral arrangement is not open to investigation, is any *academic* purpose served by continuing the sort of study in which Mr Butler, and others, are engaged?

There is here a point of fundamental importance. Journalists and politicians may want convenient handbooks; but dons are under no obligation to provide them. Increased public knowledge of the details of recent politics may flow as a by-product from works of academic enquiry: but that ought not to be the object in writing or a guide in selecting material. Even at the higher reaches of historical writing, when documents were available and archives open, conflict of interpretation is possible; the emphasis given by one writer selecting with one aim in mind will be different from the emphasis given by another. Nevertheless, when the papers are

---

[1] David Butler, *The Study of Political Behaviour* (1958), p. 21.

available and archives open, deficiencies in understanding are a result of historical blindness or academic incompetence; and the limitations imposed on the exercise of historical insight are the work of the historian by whom they are used. The assumptions of Dr Elton or Professor Trevor-Roper about the way in which events occur are no doubt arbitrary and arguable: but this does not limit their usefulness in making the historical subject-matter intelligible. Nor does it alter the fact that they, like Mr Christopher Hill and Mr Robert Blake, Dr Plumb and Mr Taylor, Mr Wormald and Dr Kenyon, work on a material which bears the weight of sustained intelligence and that Professor W. J. M. Mackenzie and Dr Robert McKenzie, Professor Birch and Mr Stewart, Mr Butler and the authors of the Annual Chatham House Surveys are working on a subject-matter which does not. And even if one must respect the integrity which prevents historians of contemporary government writing anything worthy of the name of history, many works which are designed to rescue a reputation or advance a cause (Mr Barnett's *The Desert Generals*, for example) within unacademic limits achieve greater success because they illuminate a subject-matter that is fertile. The only writing capable of explaining the characteristics of political practice emerges, in short, when high intelligence strikes life from a fruitful body of material: and it is only then (and not because the subject-matter happens to be recent and political) that political explanation is possible.

Connected with this is the habit of implying qualitative assessment of matters about which an author is inadequately informed. Of this particular temptation, the best examples will be found in the area of British government which is most effectively closed to academic scrutiny—the working of the Cabinet, the Civil Service and the House of Commons. The extensive 'pressure-group' literature may be read without discovering how far 'pressure-groups' *succeed* in influencing *government policy*, or what attitude the Cabinet, the Civil Service and M.P.'s take to direct approaches from agents of particular interests. Contemporary political science may be examined in vain for specific accounts of the working of particular cabinets or the passage of particular bills through the *private* stages to which they are subject. Yet, though the conventions of government deny them the material necessary for judgement, political scientists insist on passing judgement as though they did not. Other examples could be adduced, but one which is worthy of attention is the assessment made by Sir Ivor Jennings[1] of the part played by party in parliamentary government in Britain. Sir Ivor begins by suggesting that 'each of [the parties] has not only a policy, but a faith, doctrine or "way of life"'.[2] One need not make too heavy weather of this—except to point out that all three parties—and particularly the Conservative and Labour parties—have not *one* set of opinions which may be called 'a belief, a faith, a philosophy, a set of pre-judices or of principles' but a wide range of opinions which have been mixed together in accidental coalition as the chances of English politics, and the decisions of English politicians, have contrived. Nor need one point out too briskly, when Sir Ivor illustrates this conflict of prejudice by claiming that 'the diehards and the left wing do not understand each other because they do not speak the same language', that, amongst members of parliament, Lord Sandwich on the one hand and Mr Silverman on the other have much in common— not least because both would claim to be men of principle

<hr />

[1] Sir Ivor Jennings, *Party Politics* (1961), II, pp. 330–340.
[2] Jennings, p. 331.

and because it seems possible (to say the least) that in the House of Commons, character, manner and temperament divide or join men as much as opinion or party. However, there is an element of truth in Sir Ivor's picture at this point about which we need not argue. We need not doubt, moreover, that it is not necessary to 'take very seriously what a politician says on a public platform' (if by 'taking seriously' we mean 'if we want to find out what he really thinks'). Nor would we necessarily deny that 'much of the parliamentary programme is not contentious'[1] and that since 'other proposals are contentious because the Government has one bias and the opposition another, so that . . . a piece of legislation which either party might have introduced has particular variants to suit the "ideology" of the party in power . . . it follows that much of the Parliamentary battle is shadow boxing'. At this point, it is true, we begin to wonder whether Sir Ivor is not affecting to take the public parliamentary battle at its face value in order merely to denigrate it. This impression is confirmed by the remark that 'to make a debating point, suitable for the debating hall of the Oxford Union Society, is to get a cheer from the back benches'.[2] The impression then grows stronger. 'If the opposition sets out to be reasonable and to improve Government proposals, it is, however, not winning votes' is an observation which may or may not be true, according to the extent to which an opposition may in time win more votes by remaining silent than by pursuing the constant harrying which Sir Ivor evidently supposes to be the normal role of a parliamentary opposition. 'The real purpose of Parliamentary debate is not to help the Government but to turn it out at the next election' is true again only in some circumstances: and the assertion that 'it is a sham battle

<hr>

[1] Jennings, p. 332. [2] Jennings, p. 333.

because everybody sees that the whole purpose is "party political"' is true so long as it is made within the framework of understanding that much in Parliament is decided in private, that debate *can* affect policy and *does* affect the reputations of individual Members and Ministers, and that the 'sham battle', when combined with newspaper presentation, performs an important *public* function by focusing public attention on changes in that long process of parliamentary and bureaucratic decision which produces a government's policy. So much of what Sir Ivor says in these pages contains so strong a mixture of truth that the reader may swallow not only the truth but the misunderstanding and wilful denigration also. It is true, though not a comprehensive statement, to say that 'the active politician is very often of the debating society type'.[1] It may be reasonable to add that 'whether a proposition is true or false is to him not important' so long as this is taken to refer to his public speeches, and provided it is understood that the primarily persuasive character of public speeches is compatible with the possiblity that they may express whatever piece of the truth a speaker happens to think important at the time. Exaggeration is a vice endemic to public speaking, and a politician *may* come to 'believe in his own exaggerations'. A politician who does *may* 'go far', *may* 'be useful in Cabinet because he sees the party point of view so well' and because he 'appreciates almost by instinct what must be said to make a decision popular in the party'. Also it is the case, as Sir Ivor remarks, that 'a first class chairman or administrator, like Balfour, *may* get turned out'.[2] All these things may happen and on occasion no doubt do: but what is clear is that, so far as concerns cabinets since 1945, Sir Ivor does not know. The relationship between an M.P.'s

[1] Jennings, p. 340.   [2] Jennings, p. 340.

public, newspaper, or constituency reputation and his reputation in the House of Commons, the Cabinet, or the Civil Service, is difficult to measure and cannot be understood without close and prolonged involvement with both. Many qualities go towards the making of a successful Minister besides his public reputation, and of these an important one may well be the respect in which a man is held by his colleagues. In English politics, it is not clear to what extent public popularity (particularly when fostered, or thought to be fostered, by a politician himself) is any guarantee of success. Nor is it always the case that adherence to party 'shibboleths' is likely to ensure success in Cabinet or the respect of back-benchers. If the 'mass meeting' produces 'mob oratory', and therefore politicians who believe in their own exaggerations, 'television and wireless' (which Sir Ivor supposes to produce 'cool and rational' argument) have their own form of 'mob oratory'—the 'sweet reasonableness' (as Sir Ivor puts it) or throw-away modesty (as it might better be called) which is, as Sir Ivor remarks, one of Mr Macmillan's public contributions to English politics and which is as much, and as little, likely to corrupt the judgement of a politician as any of the speeches which would in a different age have been made from a platform.

The fact is that Sir Ivor, in expressing a preference for government by 'first class administrators or chairmen', is criticizing the public face of parliamentary government for failing to fulfil functions which the *public* face does not attempt to fulfil. The function of parliamentary debate, public speaking and the whole apparatus of party political discussion is not the expression of truth or the making of governmental decisions, but the effecting of persuasion. It is, in this country, an important factor in the process of choosing a government, and it is

28

also the way in which over the last century the acquiescence of the population has been gained in a form of polity which it might or might not, without persuasion, have accepted. Other ways of achieving acquiescence could be conceived: and the arousing of extensive public interest in political questions has, perhaps, not always been beneficial. But, whether the process is good or bad, the interest which electors are conceived to take, and which journalists do take, in the making of decisions has produced as a response this sort of public discussion.

Nor should it be supposed, as Sir Ivor appears to, that this works in one way only. It works in two ways in two senses. In the first place, if it has given demagogues the opportunity to achieve a measure of power which they might not have achieved in the eighteenth century, it is by no means clear that demagogues (like Lloyd George, for example) govern badly: and secondly, the machinery of public discussion in some directions strengthens, as much as it weakens, the stability and power of Government. Sir Ivor objects to the parliamentary battle because it is a 'sham battle', and it may be that, if too many people realize it to be a sham battle and attach importance to the fact, Parliament's standing may suffer more than hitherto. But if it is normally a sham battle, and not a real determination of the policies of Government, it nevertheless enables Governments to decide issues which call for decision much as Sir Ivor would like them decided—as a body of responsible men considering questions in the light of the relevant considerations (including, of course, party and electoral considerations), and then, through the public machinery, justifying to electors decisions they have already reached. The 'responsible men' who constitute the Cabinet are not Civil Servants: they have risen to office by interested and successful accumulation of power within the conventions of the existing party system. Over large areas of this system ministers and cabinets are, no doubt, little more than agents of permanent Civil Service opinion. Over others they are not: and important questions, about which little is known, centre around the formation of the various styles of Civil Service opinion and the relationship between the opinions of Civil Servants and the opinions of ministers. Even if the history of Civil Service opinion may in the past have been stressed too little and the importance of party opinion stressed too much, both nevertheless matter. The public language of politicians may often be empty. The newspapers may sometimes give disproportionate attention to politicians whose influence is small. The quality of politician may not always be impressive, and the need for practical compromise may limit the scope open to those who affect in public to be men of principle. There is however, no reason to suppose that Civil Service opinion is normally unanimous either, and in these circumstances the fact that ministers and cabinets chose between conflicting policies, some of which have been presented by Civil Servants, means that the power of politicians is great. Historical investigation may, when it is possible to give it, show how difficult it is to distinguish the influence of Civil Service opinion from the influence of party opinion in the formulation of policy: it may even turn out that between ministers and Civil Servants of the same age, generation and upbringing there is a greater consensus than between ministers, or between Civil Servants, whose backgrounds differ. Explanation will probably best be conducted by assuming that Britain is governed by forty or fifty men (not all of them party politicians) whose individual opinions and influence will vary on any particular question not according to formal status but according to chance, individual character and reputation, and personal and public calculation. About these questions it is impossible to write at this stage with any measure of authority: the explanatory model must for many years be rough. But that Cabinet government, especially in relation to public opinion, very closely resembles the sort of government Sir Ivor would like to see in England, and criticizes England for failing to have, is not, it is suggested, a fact which can easily be disputed.

To say this is not to say that all members of any cabinet are of high political quality. No judgement in either direction is implied. Judgements of this sort can be validated, if at all, neither by reference to newspaper reputation, nor by the sort of knowledge which Sir Ivor and the present writer have. Nor is it to say that the conduct of English government is invariably sensible, brisk or efficient. It does, however, suggest that if the present writer has no ground for making assessment of an optimistic sort, neither has Sir Ivor any business to be making explanatory remarks of a critical sort. Are there no 'intellectual heavyweights' in English government? Do other professions 'require more work and fewer words'? Dr Charles Hill was one of the most successful post-war political broadcasters: was he a good Minister or a bad one? Does Mr Duncan Sandys work hard or merely talk too much? Is Mr Macmillan a 'first-class administrator and chairman' or a sensitive party wheel-horse or a bit of both? Did Mr Selwyn Lloyd run his Civil Servants or did they run him? Are Civil Servants promoted because of their competence, or because of a combination of competence, opinion and personal acceptability? One can search Sir Ivor's writing for assessment of the quality of work done by any particular cabinet or government department, and not find it.

One can search, not only his latest volumes but also *Parliament* and *Cabinet Government* for evidence that Sir Ivor has specific knowledge of the working of recent cabinets; and one will, not surprisingly, search in vain. In England government is surround with great secrecy, its working protected from the inquisitiveness of historians and political scientists; and the first thing a political scientist should know is how little he really knows about it.

A similar difficulty confronts writers who, under an appearance of explanation, justify preferences for, for example, the sort of governmental arrangements which have obtained in England since 1945. Sometimes the persuasions are crude, the preferences naïve and the advice blatant. What academic purpose was served by the political 'declarations' which appear in the Rector of Exeter's *Inaugural Lecture*.[1] Is anything *explained* by the remark that 'I believe that [the] system of parliamentary bureaucracy, in which both elements are organically integrated and controlled by a Cabinet system, is the ideally best form of government for a modern industrial state' (p. 5)? What is meant by the assertion that 'Bureaucracy, pure and simple, is an inferior form of government' (p. 6)? Does it show anything more important than a confidence suitable to the conditions of 1945 to claim that 'the state must be able to control society' (p. 8)? Is it a comprehensive statement to say that 'the ideal bureaucrat in our system ... is the man ... who encourages the Minister always to take the initiative and the responsibility for decisions' (p. 9)? And if it be argued that the avowal that 'I believe that a Cabinet of twelve or sixteen is the best number we (sic) can choose' was pardonable at a time of great political excitement, it is possible to match this with the equally naïve and

[1] K. C. Wheare, *The Machinery of Government*. Oxford (1945).

arbitrary conclusions ten years later that 'it is the job of a committee to come to a conclusion, to decide something' and that 'if we find that . . . the committee is a mere smokescreen behind which somebody else is performing its function, we must conclude that the committee is not doing its job'.[1]

The body of Professor Wheare's work contains a description of the *structure* of the Commonwealth and the committee system in Great Britain, but its explanatory usefulness is limited by the impossibility of showing the structure at work in specific instances. Its usefulness is limited also by the assumption that advice offered on the scale on which Professor Wheare offers it—advice, for example, to 'members, and especially chairmen, of committees[2] to be on their guard . . . against conceding point after point to a persistent minority', advice[3] 'to keep experts off committees to enquire and to arrange for them to express their views as witnesses', advice,[4] even, as to whether there would not be 'some value in having in every council a sort of "steering" committee composed of the chairmen of the principle committees of the council'—that these and similar pieces of advice fulfil any academic function at all.

A further confusion arises from the tendency to set up an arbitrary norm—the opinion of the 'plain man', for example—by which to criticize or applaud an institution that is supposed to be under investigation. Professor Kelsall tells us[5] that one justification for enquiring into the social background of higher Civil Servants is that as 'the ordinary citizen knows that since the reforms of the 1870's recruitment to the main branches of the service has been by open competition amongst those with

---

[1] *Government by Committee* (1955), p. 10.   [2] *Government by Committee*, p. 93.
[3] *Government by Committee*, p. 81.   [4] *Government by Committee*, p. 199.
[5] R. K. Kelsall 'Social Background of the Higher Civil Service' in W. A. Robson (ed.): *Civil Service in Britain and France* (1956).

the requisite education and abilities ... he naturally expects, that by this time, the proportions in which higher Civil Servants are drawn from the several social strata will roughly correspond to the relative size of these strata'.[1] He tells us that since 'recent investigations in Scotland and elsewhere have shown that some two-thirds of the children with a high level of measured intelligence have fathers in the manual and routine non-manual categories ... it is a reasonable inference that ... if, in the filling of these posts there is a marked under-representation of the lower social strata, ... the interests of the Service will suffer'. He adds finally that since the lack of drive and personal vitality 'and the tendency to be out of touch with working-class problems and ignorant of recent advances in the natural and the social sciences' which critics see as prevailing limitations of the Civil Service are 'characteristic of those with a middle class up-bringing and a public school education, ... something would be gained if those in controlling positions in the Civil Service roughly reflected in their family and school background, the pattern of society as a whole'.[2] Professor Kelsall is an academic figure and one must take his writing as evidence of something. There is, however, little evidence that 'ordinary citizens' know about the reforms of the 1870's and none to support the belief that the account given of the product of middle-class education would bear investigation. Nor is there any reason to assume that 'measured intelligence' can be correlated at all readily with intelligence at work in specific situations: that it is necessarily to the 'interest of the service' (or the country) that the standard of 'measured intelligence' in the Civil Service should be higher than its existing place in the social structure permits; or that the Civil

[1] Kelsall, p. 151.   [2] Kelsall, p. 152.

34

Service will necessarily fail to perform its social function if 'there is marked under-representation' not, as Professor Kelsall puts it, 'of the lower social strata', but of Civil Servants whose *parents* belong to the 'lower social strata'. There is indeed a world, of unsubtle, untransparent assumption behind the assertion that, until a solution has been found to the 'problem' raised by the fact that 'a position of advantage [is] conferred on [sons of Doctors, Lawyers, Clergymen and Teachers] ... by having a father in one of these professions ... *true* equality of opportunity in entering these and other occupations cannot become a reality'.[1] And it is a world which would, on investigation, reveal that, Professor Kelsall's work, so far from having at this point any explanatory value, provides on the contrary no more than a specimen for explanatory investigation.

Professor Kelsall is unsubtle and Professor W. J. M. Mackenzie is not: but that does not help Professor Mackenzie to avoid temptation. When, after a show of reticence, he exposes his assumptions about the importance of free elections, they lack this necessary transparency. Whilst not mistaking 'free elections' for 'a supreme end', he yet maintains that they are 'a device of the highest value, because no one has invented a *better political contrivance* for securing in large societies ... a sentiment of popular consent and participation ... [and a means of providing] for orderly succession in government, by the peaceful transfer of authority to new rulers when the time comes for the old rulers to go, because of mortality or because of failure'.[2] It may be that a high degree of consent and a ready transition from one régime to another is sometimes ensured by, among other things, 'free elections', but

---

[1] Kelsall in D. V. Glass: *Social Mobility in Britain* (1954), pp. 319–20.
[2] W. J. M. Mackenzie, *Free Elections* (1958), pp. 13–14.

35

there is no reason to suppose that these consequences can be correlated to the electoral system alone. Nor is there any reason to suppose that electors reject governments because of 'failure' in performing the central duties of government. The reasons which move voters to vote (if put beside a government's actual conduct) probably bear little looking into. Governments which have 'succeeded' (in an administrative or governmental sense) may nevertheless 'fail' in an electoral sense; and there is no reason to suppose that electors can judge the first with any serious precision. Governments chosen by 'free elections' may sometimes be better than others; but there is unlikely to be a high correlation (if measurement of this kind can be made at all) between a part of the process by which men come to office (a free election) and the use they make of office once they get it.

Those who understand this point may warm to Professor Mackenzie's admission that 'there are extremities which require the old Roman proclamation of executive rule'. They should, however, not be disarmed, for it prefaces the arbitrary assertion that 'the doctrine of responsibility to an electorate is the best for electoral use'—an assertion which is persuasive rather than explanatory, and which is systematically misleading when it is said to be so 'because it is the *only* available guarantee of consent and continuity in government'.[1] More than definition is involved here. It could be that Professor Mackenzie intends only a definition when he says that 'all governments, if not foolishly conducted, have regard to opinion: democratic governments rest on consent'.[2] It seems, however, more likely that he supposes the relationship between governments and subjects in democratic societies to have a quality which others have not. Is this

[1] Mackenzie, p. 14.   [2] Mackenzie, p. 175.

so, however? Is the relationship between government and subjects in societies where elections are not free significantly different from the relationship in societies where they are? Professor Mackenzie makes something of the idea that 'an election confers legitimate authority', but is this true? Elections are part of the process by which parliaments and ministers emerge: but it is not adequate to say that elections 'confer authority'. Governments can be equally legitimate where no election has occurred, or where election is not part of the normal political process. 'Free elections', 'muddled elections', 'stolen elections', 'made elections', and 'elections by acclamation' all in their various ways play a conventional part in the societies in which they occur. To set up a universal standard of suitability is useless: and where one finds a 'pathology' mentioned in this connection and a 'recognizable norm . . . and different patterns of departure from it', one must conclude that Professor Mackenzie, instead of engaging in a purely explanatory study, is at this point persuading, by exaggeration, to admiration of what may be called Western-democratic political arrangements.

Finally, one may agree when Professor Robson justifies his dismissal of some criticisms of bureaucracy by claiming that 'nothing fruitful is likely to emerge from an attitude which postulates that the best method of solving the problems of public administration in the welfare state is to put the clock back a hundred years and return to the halcyon days when the executive did almost nothing judged by modern standards'.[1] Agreement, however, need not stop one adding that nothing academically fruitful is likely to come from uncritically enunciating such slogans as that 'bureaucracy is clearly indispensable to modern government . . .

[1] W. A. Robson, op. cit. p. 5.

because it uses objective methods of recruitment in place of nepotism ... seeks to promote according to merit rather than for political or personal reasons ... administers on the basis of rules, precedents and policy rather than on grounds of personal feelings, influence or favouritism'.[1] 'Bureaucracy', or at any rate a strong Civil Service, may well have been indispensable to the sort of government Professor Robson wanted in 1947: but not for the reason he gives. Is it, one may ask, a more 'objective' method of recruitment to choose candidates through special interview and written examination than by some other test of suitability? Do 'personal reasons' not affect the promotion of Civil Servants? Did the Crichel Down episode show Civil Servants administering without reference to 'personal feelings'? and is it conceivable that they should? The Civil Service, in fact, in these respects is little different from any other institution: and there is no need to offer, as a contribution to Political Science, statements which present as matters of fact what are little more than hopeful intentions.

If the objection to the passages quoted from Sir Ivor Jennings is that their author, whilst understanding that the Cabinet's first function is to govern, knows too little to justify assessment of its competence, there is a parallel objection to the habit of extracting from the living body of a social institution readily accessible quantitative facts and supposing that they explain the working of the institution as a whole. Measurement of the quality of life produced by the various social institutions is the most difficult of all the burdens assumed by the student of the social sciences. Yet to those who, like Professor Macrae, assume that an important professional function is to assist in the amelioration of society, it ought surely to be the point at which greatest care is taken to ensure

[1] Robson, p. 2.

38

that the material under discussion can yield the sort of evidence it is supposed to yield. If amelioration of society is a concern of the social scientist, then he should study not just what it is easy to discover (because the material is measurable) but the whole impact an institution leaves in performing the central function for which it is intended. Much attention of late has been given to English education. The primary purpose of education is to teach whatever skills are necessary to the maintenance of society and to sharpen, and intensify, the quality of mind with which the whole population approaches the task of living. Yet one may search the pages of Messrs Young, Collier, Furneaux, Vaisey, Glass and Pedley for assessment of the quality of mind induced by existing educational arrangements. Interesting facts emerge—about the level of educational expenditure, about mobility between classes, about the social value of the public schools, about the 'new élite' and about the range of employment open to the varying classes. Many sorts of comment and information are offered which will support a radical concern with social equality. But too little is said (except by Mr Holbrook) about the increase or diminution of those sorts of intelligence which do not connect with this particular concern and nothing of consequence about the quality of the impact made by the schools on the nation's intellectual life.

Not that the few attempts which are made at general qualitative assessment are always successful. Professor Marshall is a widely respected sociologist: but it is difficult to take seriously the claims he makes about the joint impact of planning and sociology on British education. 'We used', he wrote in his *Inaugural Lecture*, 'to find the class of school children treated as an undifferentiated mass, with a single mind and a single voice, chanting its lessons in unison. At the other end of the scale was the view that each child should be regarded as a unique personality from which the teacher must draw out and develop the gifts planted there by nature. ... The choice seemed to lie between a heap of stones and a battery of test tubes. But today we see the class as a living group with an educative force of its own, and recognise that the development of a child that is to become a social being must take place within the field of action and reaction that such a group creates. The nature of these intra-group relations is one of the main objects of sociological study. There is also the problem of integrating life in the school with life outside. If a sharp dichotomy exists, the child must change role with the skill of a professional actor as he passes from home to classroom. ... This analysis of the child ... is yielding to a synthesis which has, I believe, already, affected the attitude of children towards those schools. Finally there is the biggest problem of all, the adjustment of education to meet the needs of life in a changing society. It is, therefore, by no means inappropriate that an eminent sociologist should have been appointed to the Chair of Education in the University of London.'[1]

In another passage the same scholar, after sketching the history of the 'extension of the social services' in the last fifty years, observes that this is 'not primarily a means of equalising incomes' but a means for 'a general enrichment of the concrete substance of civilised life'.[2] One can agree that there *is* a 'general reduction of risk and insecurity' and this *may* be thought of as part of a 'general enrichment of the concrete substance of civilised life'. It is, however, far from clear that 'equalisation between the ... healthy and the sick, the employed and the unemployed, the old and the active,

[1] T. H. Marshall, *Sociology at the Crossroads* (1947), pp. 14–15.
[2] *Citizenship and Social Class* (1950), p. 56.

the bachelor and the father of a large family' constitutes 'enrichment' of this sort. Is any sort of 'general
enrichment' to be found in (and, indeed, what is one
to make of Professor Marshall's solemnity about) the
fact that in the Welfare State all citizens have 'a new
common experience'—the 'common experience' of
learning 'what it means to have an insurance card that
must be regularly stamped (by somebody)'. If it is
unreasonable to object when scholars appoint themselves laureates of the Welfare State, this passage suggests
that there ought, at least, to be minimal awareness of the
fact that not all its aspects need be defended as
necessary consequence of a categorical imperative.

It may be objected that what is being asked for is too
difficult for an academic study to undertake: and that
is, indeed, the point that is being urged. If measurement
could be made (and once made, could be agreed) about
the quality of education in English schools, then the
practical injunctions of scholars would begin to have
authority. But can conclusions which take no account of
the most important element in the activity carry
binding authority at all? And if it is difficult to obtain a
comprehensive view of the quality of our educational
system, is not something to be said for abandoning the
academic attempt altogether? In practice and explanation equally selection is necessary: and no selection can
be more than temporary and tentative. But, just as
selection which advances explanation may be unhelpful
in practice, so selection with a view to practice may
hamper explanation.

Indeed, if practice were to wait on explanation, action
would never be taken. One facet of the academic
dialectic, a desirable consequence of academic irresponsibility, is that there is about any particular explanation a
sort of infinite regress, so that as soon as its author has

reached the point at which it seems coherent and comprehensive to him, others expose the arbitrariness and abridgement on which it is built. Sometimes the abridgement takes unexpected shape. When Professor MacKinnon stresses the existential quality of 'revolt', his words seem powerful. But they seem less so when we reflect that 'obedience' has existential quality also, and that to impute to 'revolt' in general a peculiarly heightened quality of 'being', is to distort the character of existence by attending to only a part of it. In reporting the stimulus he has received from existentialist discussion, Professor MacKinnon, it is true, so far from claiming for its insights the status of professional moral philosophy 'at any rate as it is practiced in these islands', recognizes rather that 'they supply matter for the comment of the professional political philosopher, matter which is particularly welcome when it would seem that academic moral philosophy is beginning to concern itself again with the images men form of the life they believe themselves called upon to try to lead'.[1] This, however, though cautious does not help Professor MacKinnon over the obvious obstacle. When he asserts that the language of revolt, rebellion or protest (as manifested, for example, in the 'neutralism . . . so . . . abhorred by State Department and Pentagon') in order to be 'protest' rather than 'escapism' must be 'in the name of natural law', one is aware of the density of the concept. Many things are done, and many claims made, 'in the name of natural law' which it cannot be assumed that the 'natural law' guarantees. And this is so whether 'natural law' is taken to mean 'a catena of supposedly self-evident propositions' or 'a form of life which at once constrains and attracts men unconditionally'. In practice commands which 'constrain and attract men unconditionally'

[1] 'Existentialism and Revolt', *Cambridge Opinion*, XXIV, p. 20.

almost certainly will be supported by what seem to the actor 'self-evident propositions', but that does not guarantee that they are. The 'name of natural law', the sense of 'self-evidence' and the 'unconditional constraint' provide no guarantee that right is being done or the 'natural law' pursued: nor do they ensure that 'revolt' or 'rebellion' have an unconditionally meritorious quality absent from 'obedience', 'conformity' or the tendency to reject 'revolt', 'protest' or 'rebellion'.

Professor MacKinnon is less than fair to those who choose not to protest and shows no grasp of the similarity between the existential status of 'revolt' and the existential status of 'obedience'. If it is true that 'the category of revolt throws into very clear relief the creative quality of the individual', it is equally true that many other sorts of action do also. The alternative suggested by those who oppose American nuclear policy cannot usefully be characterized as a 'confused sense that life should have more to offer than submission to the sovereignty of American global strategy'. 'Life' certainly does have 'more to offer' than this: and will continue to do so in its manifold ways whether Britain or the United States have nuclear weapons or not. It might, with as good reason, be replied that those who support a nuclear N.A.T.O. do so out of a confused sense that 'life should have more to offer than submission to the sovereignty of *Russian* global strategy'. One might remark seriously, where Professor MacKinnon remarks ironically, that 'what was done by the Western Powers at Hiroshima and Nagasaki, and the preparations which led up to these events, were the work of men who claimed to represent the traditions of the Christian West'; and one might add that Germans who showed what Professor MacKinnon calls 'the more obvious

43

responses invited by the situation in Germany in 1942' (instead of scribbling slogans on walls, as the Munich students did in their 'existential protest') were doing right according to the 'unconditional constraints' to which their own conception of duty moved them.

Almost anything Professor MacKinnon says about 'revolt' may be said about other attitudes also. Although he was at liberty for practical purposes to attempt to persuade the audience he was addressing that *revolt* provides unique opportunities for the operation of moral worth, mere appropriation of the language of 'Being' does not elevate *his* opinion above any other. Nor does appropriation of the language of 'existence' necessarily meet the metaphysical requirement, advance conformity to the natural law or succeed more completely than any other action in doing God's Will or accomplishing his purposes. And if the literature of revolt does in fact provide (as it certainly does) occasion for the 'comment of the moral philosopher', the chief comment the moral philosopher must take is that, since the language of revolt has the same existential status as any other sort of language and since to impute to revolt a heightened status is to abridge 'Being', *his* sort of comment is unlikely to be helpful in providing binding commands to action.

The fourth confusion to which attention must be drawn is a tendency to suppose that the history of political thought is more likely than other sorts of historical writing to throw light on the nature of political activity in general. When historians of thought show the changes wrought in the most carefully formulated ideas once they leave the hands of their originators, then much light is shed. When the writings of earlier political philosophers are studied in the framework of the

44

society or tradition in which they lived (so as to explain how far they were helped, or hindered, in their description of reality by the distortions which came from living when they did) historical work can be done. In fact, however, the historian of ideas has not seldom become one because he would like to contribute to political reflection (but lacks the equipment to take off). Too much attention is given to articulate political philosophers and too little to the connection between political ideas and the history of society as a whole. Mr Parkin's *The Moral Basis of Burke's Political Thought* would be better history if it explained how Burke emerged from English history and better philosophy if, as well as explaining what Burke meant, it asked whether what Burke meant was sensible. Professor Stokes's *The English Utilitarians and India* would gain greatly from asking what factors besides doctrine made the Government of India act as it did, while Mr Kedourie's *England and the Middle East 1914–21* (which is a subtle study of ideas affecting political practice) would be subtler still if his subject could be followed in diplomatic detail from fully-opened archives.

Even when philosophical competence is not in doubt, the results are not always happy. Cassirer's *The Philosophy of the Enlightenment*, for example, is a major work; but it nowhere suggests that the greatest victories of the Enlightenment were won not by the great eighteenth-century figures with whom its pages are filled but by obscure publishers and obscurer schoolmasters who in the last century and a half have inoculated a wider audience with a vulgar version of the ideas these figures were the first to shape. Accounts, in a manner neither historical nor philosophical, of the political doctrines of highly articulate men are interesting objects of study, but (in *The Open Society and its Enemies*) extremely misleading

45

ones. Total historical explanation is difficult to achieve except for the most limited topic over the most limited period. To understand not just what Marx, Plato or Hegel said but also the use they made of the materials they had to hand is one of the most difficult exercises of the historical imagination. It demands an unusual combination of biographical detail and intellectual grip, but is rewarding because a man's merit cannot be ascertained, even as imperfectly as it can be, unless detailed work is undertaken. Even if it can be achieved only rarely, however, a little of it would be far more illuminating than the large acres of unfruitful chronicle where the great political writers sit contemplating their great political thoughts or being alternately praised and blamed for their portentous political effects without any hint that a devious world is often less interested, and less respectful, than it might be.

There is a style of historico-philosophical writing of great and respectable authority which shows how political philosophers in the past succeeded in reaching a plateau of intelligibility which can be judged without reference to the circumstances in which they wrote. Much fine and intelligent criticism of this sort has been written. It is illuminating to see his *History of Philosophy* showing how Hegel imagined himself to have drawn together the conflicting strands in European philosophy: or Professor Gilson's *Spirit of Mediaeval Philosophy* showing how the perennial problems of philosophy were dealt with, and dealt with, he suggests, rightly, by mediaeval theologians. This manner of writing has value and validity: but falls short of being philosophy because it deals only by implication with the problems with which philosophy has to deal and falls short of being history because it fails to set the thought of the philosopher in the context of the society in which he

46

lived. Philosophers live in an intellectual tradition as well as in a personal situation. Political philosophers live also in particular political societies with involved histories and complicated commitments of their own: and the tendency of the philosopher's history of philosophy is to stress the first and neglect the second.

A temptation, furthermore, is strong amongst a group of historical moralists to suggest that certain manners of political thinking and certain modes of political expression are bad because of the consequences they produce in practice. Writers who maintain exaggerated expectations about the consequences of political action are supposed to do damage to the structure of society as a whole. A scapegoat has been constructed by Professor Talmon which professes to account for the history of Europe since 1789—a scapegoat of rationalistic utopianism so destructive of settled political habits as to be responsible not just for intellectual misunderstanding but for political consequences in a way which can be avoided in the future. Occamist Nominalism in the hands of Professor Weaver[1] and Cartesian Dualism in those of Miss Arendt,[2] Platonic Idealism with Professor Popper[3] and Hegel's Idealism with Hobhouse[4]—are used to show a similar foreshortening of historical perspective by attributing to a false philosophy the disorders of a civilization which (if they are agreed to exist at all) are so extensive and profound that it is incredible they should have arisen from so limited a source.

It may be urged that Professor Talmon understands the limitations of his work: but his words give no ground for thinking that he does. His prefatory caution provides,

[1] R. M. Weaver, *Ideas Have Consequences* (1948).
[2] Hannah Arendt, *The Human Condition* (1958).
[3] K. R. Popper, *The Open Society and Its Enemies* (1945).
[4] L. T. Hobhouse, *The Metaphysical Theory of the State* (1918).

no doubt, some measure of excuse for the assertion[1] that 'from the vantage point of the mid-twentieth century, the history of the last 150 years looks like a *systematic* [my italic] preparation for the head-long collision between empirical and liberal democracy on the one hand and totalitarian Messianic democracy on the other in which the world crisis of today consists'. Professor Talmon writes, however, so much from within the tradition of thinking he is describing that it is not clear when he is explaining the tradition itself and when he is taking part in its own internal discussion. What, for example, is meant by the sentence: 'Totalitarian democracy early evolved into a pattern of coercion and centralisation not because it rejected the values of eighteenth-century liberal individualism, but because it had originally a too perfectionist attitude towards them'?[2] Does this mean that those whom Professor Talmon calls 'totalitarian democrats' advocated measures of 'coercion and centralisation' or does it mean that their style of thinking produced, not by intention but as a political by-product, 'coercion and centralisation'. On page 250 it seems that Professor Talmon means the former: on page 251 the latter. But if it is the latter, then the body of his text does not establish it. Since many other factors besides doctrine helped to produce coercion between 1789 and 1795, no conclusion of relevance to the doctrines can be deduced from consideration of the tangled and unsatisfactory circumstances in which some of those who maintained them found themselves involved in practice. But if the political consequences cannot be correlated so simply to the writings of those who make an impact on them, can Professor Talmon's *conclusions* carry practical authority at all?

[1] J. L. Talmon, *Origins of Totalitarian Democracy* (ed. 1961), p. 1.
[2] Talmon, p. 249.

It is reasonable to suggest that the 'messianic utopians' were wrong in supposing that, given a combination of revolutionary conditions, good intentions and adequate doctrine, all political difficulties could be resolved. History provides no lessons: but it certainly shows that optimism of this kind is not armoured with built-in guarantees against disappointment. But this is a negative conclusion, and history itself will carry us no further. Professor Talmon, however, attempts to go further. 'The tracing of the genealogy of ideas' may, as he claims, provide an opportunity 'for stating some conclusions of a general nature'[1]: but if the conclusions are practical ones, then there is no more intimate connection between the genealogy and the conclusions than the fact that Professor Talmon has put them together in the same cover. Does the *historical* investigation establish that 'the most important lesson to be drawn from [it] is the incompatibility of the idea of an all-embracing and all-solving creed with liberty'? Is the 'attempt to satisfy both [i.e. the yearning for salvation and the desire for freedom] at the same time ... *bound* [my italic] to result, if not in unmitigated tyranny and serfdom, at least in the monumental hypocrisy of self-deception which are the concomitants of totalitarian democracy'? Is the general political structure of any society ever the result simply of the doctrines held by those who exercise power within it? Even the most messianically-inspired theorist, once confronted with the chance to exercise power, is likely to be faced with, and to face, problems connected with the survival of his régime, and these problems will affect his action quite as much as the doctrines in which he believes. Even if it were true that the 'reign of the exclusive, yet all-solving, doctrine of totalitarian

---

[1] Talmon, p. 253.

democracy runs counter to the lessons of nature and history'[1] because 'nature and history' (though not, as it happens, Professor Talmon's book) 'show civilisation as the evolvement of a multiplicity of historically and pragmatically formed clusters of social existence', there would be as much, and as little, sense in replying that the lessons of 'nature and history' show also that, if men do not in practice believe in some 'exclusive, all-embracing creed', they are unlikely to achieve anything of consequence, and will certainly not advance civilization or the progress of their own societies to any significant extent.

It may be useful in explanation to urge, as Professor Talmon does, that 'it is a harsh, but none the less necessary, task to drive home the truth that human society and human life can never reach a state of repose'. It is not a truth of explanation, however, but a practical persuasion which does not at all follow to add that 'all that can be done is to proceed by the method of trial and error'.[2] Men do proceed in other ways: and, even if they will not necessarily achieve what they want, the history Professor Talmon is writing produces no binding reason why they should not continue to think that they might. Professor Talmon supposes that 'like a psychoanalyst who cures by making the patient aware of his sub-conscious, the social analyst may be able to attack the human urge which calls totalitarian democracy into existence, namely the longing for a final resolution of all contradictions . . . into a state of total harmony', but one can only observe that men will probably go on feeling this urge whatever the social analyst may say. Nothing in Professor Talmon's history justifies the belief that men who suppose themselves to be searching for this sort of political harmony produce consequences necessarily

[1] Talmon, p. 254. [2] Talmon, pp. 254–5.

worse than those who suppose that it can never be reached at all. Professor Talmon is untransparent at this important point because he uses an abstraction from a past which is more complicated than he recognizes in order to impute to his favoured style of politics—a liberal, pragmatic one, as it happens—a superior practical suitability which *explanation* provides no reason to think it has.

Burke's was the most extended attempt to impute to utopian language an outcome as disastrous as the language was wicked, and to attach to passing intellectual positions the disagreeable consequences which follow when a whole society falls apart. Robespierre, Mirabeau and the other revolutionary leaders combined in their characters no more than a recognizable combination of ambition, ignorance, dishonesty and recklessness characteristic of those who come to power in revolutionary situations. They enunciated foolish slogans about political action which must have had *some* effect on the way in which they worked. But it is idle to blame them for revolution or revolutionary wars whose roots will be found in many factors beside the language they used: and ridiculous to draw the conclusion that, if *their* pretensions had been avoided, the consequences would necessarily have been better. If the monarchy had not failed, they would never have exercised power at all: and it is doubtful whether men who had never had the chance to exercise power before would, in the situation with which they were faced, have controlled events more efficiently if the political handbooks they had read had been more sensible. It was as foolish to impute to the revolutionaries full responsibility for their actions as it was to credit the Revolution of 1688 with the agreeable consequence of stabilizing the State. The Revolution of 1688 was as complicated a conjunction of interests, betrayals and fears as any revolution that has ever occurred, and the stability of late eighteenth-century English society was the result not just of one event or another and not just of one interest or another, but, as Burke perfectly well knew, of the whole course of eighteenth-century history.

It is not suggested that the doctrine of 'positive liberty' had no political consequences. Nor is it denied that Professor Talmon and Sir Isaiah Berlin perform a valuable service in constructing scapegoats and abridging history in order to expose the inadequacy of the illusion that European politics was in some sense all wrong before 1789 and became very much better thereafter. Whatever their merits, however, these writers, and writers like them, are responsible for a serious error. They imply that Europe's difficulties in the last century and a half have arisen chiefly from philosophical misconceptions and they have, therefore, fired salvoes at the consequences of political doctrines which could, with academic advantage, have been fired in different directions. Instead of supposing that they have traced the consequences of utopian doctrines in the political *practice* of Europe, which they do not in fact do, they would have done better to consider their consequences in political philosophy. They ought either to give detailed accounts of particular political situations (where thought can be seen limited by action) or to explain what political activity is like looked at in the framework of the whole of existence. Abridgement, even with goodwill, is dangerous. History, without the detail, is misleading: it tends, whilst professing to present the history of an institution or situation, to describe only the opinions held by those responsible for exercising power within it. The difficulty in the way of doing anything else, where the subject-matter is vast, is immense, but this does not make it less necessary to do it. Works which, like Mr E. H. Carr's, claim to be a *History of the Russian Revolution* but give only an account of the view of one set of participants positively damage understanding. Vast scholarly edifices, like Dr Ullmann's *The Growth of Papal Government in the Middle Ages*, which attempt to trace the development of papal government and yet give, chiefly, an account of the history of the 'principles' on which papal government was 'based',[1] positively conceal the tension between doctrine and action characteristic of such histories. Whole volumes of writing in this manner can be read without finding out what happened, without, indeed, finding out anything more than what men thought had happened in the past or what they said should happen in the future. Even where this is as massive, necessary and self-confident a stage in the development of historical writing as Dr Ullmann makes it, it is, as history, so incomplete as to hamper explanation. History, properly executed, should reveal mind unsatisfied with its surrounding, thought cheated and men wrestling with the difficulties of the world. But it is only when circumstance as well as thought, its limitations as well as mind, are revealed that the scapegoats of the European consciousness (Occam or Descartes, Kant or Rousseau, Hegel, Machiavelli or Marx, according to one's preference) can be held responsible, not for the distant consequences of their followers' actions, but solely for the direction of their thought.

Fifthly, there is the temptation to use large words like 'freedom', 'social justice', 'the national interest', 'rational', 'values' and 'international understanding' as though they have self-evident moral content apart from the situations to which they might be applied or as

[1] W. Ullmann, p. v.

though, once they have been applied to particular situations, they are likely to retain very much content at all. 'Values' are what people parade who have neither settled habits nor religion to tell them how to act. In all these things 'good' can seldom be achieved except by action which some people think bad. To give freedom to one group almost always involves restricting the freedom of another. Freedom to vote (when given to people, in Africa, for example, who do not have it) can hardly fail to mean that people who have the vote already will carry less weight in the government of their country in the future. Freedom for all opinions to be expressed may mean that those who perform useful or profitable functions without bothering to be articulate about them will be subjected to criticism, attack and expropriation. The increase of 'international understanding' (which is supposed to assist reconciliation between nations) may not infrequently, by revealing the true objectives of all, increase the hostility which each feels for the others. 'Social justice' often involves taxing one group in order to provide goods for another. The 'national interest' may mean the interest of the nation as judged by those who have authority to decide it or may merely be an interest which uses an impressive adjective to advance its own power: the ambiguity of the phrase should not conceal the fact that changes can be no less arbitrary (or unpredictable) when they are effected in its name. The chief consequence of the belief which has grown up in the last fifty years that governments have a duty to supervise British industry 'in the national interest' has been to create an interest of this sort—an interest of public relations advisers, trade associations and industrial federations enjoying considerable influence in defending productive industries from opposing groups of political manipulators, public servants and progressive publicists who make this influence possible by advocating extensive governmental intervention.

Professor Titmuss, for example, may, if he wants to, stigmatize as 'arbitrary' the distribution of economic power in contemporary England and imply that a properly regulated 'social conscience' will want to alter it.[1] 'Arbitrary' is a useful word but in this context what does it mean? Obviously not that directors of insurance companies owe no account to anyone or are totally irresponsibile: for they have, as Professor Titmuss recognizes, considerable responsibility, and an extensive interest in ensuring that the money they invest is not used on undertakings that fail. Also, in an important sense, their power is no more arbitrary than that of Professor Titmuss, who would resent the suggestion that Parliament, the Ministry of Education or the Chairman of the British Employers' Confederation should be given responsibility to scrutinize his lectures. Nevertheless, it does seem to mean that insurance companies owe no account to Parliament, the Civil Service or Professor Titmuss and that Professor Titmuss would like them to: which, though open to objection, is a possible position to adopt—provided it is recognized to be merely his opinion and not the conclusion of political science: and so long as it is not implied that those who reach different conclusions necessarily do so by subordinating considera- tion of the merits of the question to self-interest or personal ambition. About the practical direction of affairs, even where there is agreement about ends, there is usually disagreement about means: and since neither means nor ends are usually agreed by general consensus, it would be wrong for the philosopher to claim any sort of certainty for any of them. Everybody recognizes that good should be done: but not everybody agrees what

[1] R. M. Titmuss, *The Irresponsible Society* (1960), p. 3.

good it should be. The principle of utility, the march of history and the natural law have in different places been taken as binding standards by which action should be judged. But the principle of utility, the march of history and the natural law command universally to nothing: and to claim that they do neither insulates against disagreement nor provides any greater authority than the hunches and commitments which are mixed in all political judgement with 'personal' ambition, 'selfish' interest and 'prudential' calculation. Utility *and* history, tradition *and* the moral will, benevolence *and* interest, prudence *and* duty are all capable of suggesting what it is right to do: and only a confused philosopher will suggest that one principle can be known necessarily to be more reasonable than these others.

Lord Russell, in defending the use of 'reason' in politics, writes that ' "Reason" has a perfectly clear and precise meaning. It signifies the choice of the right means to the end that you wish to achieve . . .' and he adds that 'if I wish to travel by plane to New York, reason tells me that it is better to take a plane which is going to New York than one which is going to Constantinople.'[1] One may accept that as a reasonable statement. Nevertheless, it hardly amounts to a political example: it concerns the achievement by one man of a limited objective, not the achievement by many men, or a whole society, of objectives as diffuse and general as the maintenance of peace or the avoidance of self-destruction. Indeed, if one were to ask how a man should conduct himself so as to live as long as it is possible, given his existing temperament and constitution, to live, it is far from certain that an answer as clear and straightforward as 'taking a plane to New York instead of to Constantinople' would be sufficient. And if this is true of an

[1] Bertrand Russell, *Human Society in Ethics and Politics* (1954), p. 8.

56

individual man, it is much more true of a whole society or of all the societies which constitute a civilization. One may agree with Lord Russell that 'never before has man as man been in danger from nuclear weapons', but what are we to make of the conclusion to which his 'reason' has come as to the means to be pursued in order to avoid the danger—that 'if men are to escape from the consequences of their own cleverness, they will have to learn, in all the powerful countries of the world ... to think, not of separate groups of men, but of MAN', 'to replace the old crude passions of hate and greed and envy by a new wisdom based upon the realization of our common danger' and that 'the only thing that will redeem mankind is co-operation'?[1] Not very much, it may be said: but if attention is given to the more detailed conclusions to which Lord Russell's reason has led him, greater precision will be found. In Chapter 9 of the same work, Lord Russell attempts to ask the question 'how is the fanaticism of those who rule in the U.S.A. and U.S.S.R. to be prevented from doing its evil work?' The removal of mutual fear is assumed to be the first obstacle to be dealt with and the 'low level rationality' (by which the two sets of rulers, living in their balance-of-power nightmare, are said to be moved) overcome by 'conciliation ... and a gradual diminution of hate and fear' (and, presumably, by 'rationality' of a higher order). Here one might expect to find a conclusion of great consequence, here if anywhere an answer which would do something to save the world. But all in fact we find is that Lord Russell wishes to 'see the Government of India appoint a Commission, consisting solely of Indians ... to investigate in a wholly neutral spirit the evils to be expected if the cold war becomes hot'.[2]

[1] Russell, pp. 211–12.   [2] Russell, p. 231.

About this it is necessary to say three things. First, that it hardly seems necessary to call in the Indian Government to remind politicians of wide experience that nuclear weapons can damage them as well as other people. And if it *is* necessary (because they are mad), then 'impartial reasonableness' is unlikely to make any impact anyway. Nuclear war has not occurred since 1945 (or since Lord Russell wrote in 1954). This provides no guarantee for the future: but the dramatic dangers which face the world ought not to conceal the fact that calculated self-interest has almost certainly mitigated the chauvinism of the leaders of both great blocs in the last fifteen years. Secondly, there is no reason to think that the Indian, or any other, Government could in any useful sense be 'neutral'. The Indian Government has interests of its own (in Kashmir for example), in pursuing which Mr Nehru's reputation as a world mediator who will not for long offend any of the Great Powers plays a part. A commission might not be able to produce an agreed report: but if it did, the language in which it would be written, the blame it imputed to the various governments and the implications its recommendations would have for their interests would mean that, instead of being treated as 'reason's' judgement of the problem, it would, like all other political documents, be used to snatch whatever advantage the various Powers could snatch for their several interests. Thirdly, remembering Lord Russell's definition of reason as 'choice of the right means to the end that you wish to achieve', one may ask by what authority Lord Russell's is taken to be the right means to achieve the end he wishes to achieve. Even if Lord Russell could provide assurances about the use to which the Powers would put the commission, it is reasonable to suggest that many other courses of action would be as likely to

58

keep the peace as any of the alternatives he might be likely to suggest. It would be absurd to state that Lord Russell is demonstrably wrong to prefer *his* policy to the policy of working through existing diplomatic machinery. It is, however, equally absurd to claim for his views about a complicated situation greater 'rationality' than for any others, or to imagine that his political assertions are anything more than persuasions to action with all the uncertainty and indeterminate rationality which such statements almost invariably have.

It is important to make clear what is not being suggested. Advice that is buttressed by words like 'reason' or 'natural law' is not necessarily wrong, nor has the philosopher any obligation to prevent them being used. In practice they *are* used, and the philosopher's task is to explain that this is so. But if it is beyond his competence to suggest that they ought not to play a part in practice, it is essential to his function to make clear that they have no necessary standing in explanation. And this is so whatever the tradition of thinking from which the word comes. 'The Categorical Imperative' has the same status as the 'Natural Law' and the 'Will of God' as the 'Principle of Utility'. The tendency to claim Divine Sanction for particular lines of political action in no way removes them from explanatory judgement. Dr Munby[1]—in rejecting the 'pietist delusion' that there are no Christian social principles and in attempting to give specific practical content to them, tells us that 'people require to be assured that they can, sooner or later, find a job more or less appropriate to their abilities' and that 'with a proper full employment policy, there is no problem in meeting this need'.[2] It is, however, not clear in what mood we are to suppose that 'require' is to be taken.

[1] *God and the Rich Society* (1961), p. 131. [2] Munby, pp. 33-4.

59

The statement looks at first sight explanatory: but is it? Certainly many people do expect 'society', 'the Government' or a firm to provide them with employment of a sort: though, equally, others realize that they have to find, or make, employment for themselves. It is much less clear that people *expect* to find a job 'more or less appropriate to their talents', though no doubt many who have jobs to which little social esteem is attached *hope* that they will find better ones in future. It is true also that, in periods of inflation, the maintenance of high employment presents no difficulty (so long as this question is isolated from more general questions concerning relations between management and trade unions, and so long as questions are not asked about the quality of work produced in societies whose governments give highest priority to maintaining full employment). Even if these points are accepted, however, it shows insensitivity to the complications involved in fitting people 'according to their abilities' to imply either that it is not difficult or that the consequences can easily be measured. The more closely one looks at this statement as a contribution to explanation, the clearer it becomes that Dr Munby has adopted the working practical assumptions which are used in official discussion today, and attributed to them an explanatory merit they do not have. There can be no objection to Dr Munby believing full employment to be desirable. But if Dr Munby imagines that his statement is an explanatory one, then those who are concerned with explanation must reply that it is not.

What is the status of Dr Munby's assertions that 'God does not seek glory in circumscribing the actions of men', that 'gross differences in income between people in one society are to be condemned out of hand'[1]

[1] *Christianity and Economic Problems*, pp. 119–20.

60

and that 'the enlargement of human choice, whether through an expanding economy or through the discoveries of science or art or literature, is all part of God's design for men'?[1] Dr Munby has already admitted that 'it has sometimes appeared in the history of the Christian Church as if the Christian religion were ill-disposed towards the pretensions of men to exercise choice' and has described the 'peculiar perversions of the Christian faith to which both Catholicism and Calvinism have tended to succumb'[2] in thinking that 'from the platitude that human choice provides both the opportunity for, and the sole occasion of, sin, the dangerous practical maxim [may be drawn] that human choice is to be limited and restricted, whether by the inquisition or the Kirk Session, so that the greater glory may be given to God by thus restricting the manifestations of sin'. But, if men have earnestly and honestly deduced these opinions from their Christian allegiance, by what *reasoning* can Dr Munby's contrary certainty be supported. In a passage in an earlier book he rightly observes that 'the assertions of the Christian faith about man are not simple statements of fact but metaphysical assertions ... which cannot be tested as to their truth by the ordinary methods of testing'.[3] If this is so, however, and if one may agree with Dr Munby that 'with this sort of assertion, there is not the same difficulty in deducing imperatives ... because these statements contain a hidden imperative in them', it is necessary also to add that this is not the whole difficulty. About the practical content of the meta-physical imperative, opinions are likely to differ, and, for practical purposes, these differences can be resolved, if they have to be resolved at all, only by *authoritative*

[1] *God and the Rich Society*, p. 43.   [2] *God and the Rich Society*, p. 42.
[3] *Christianity and the Economic Problem* (1956), p. 22.

decision. Dr Munby, on the same page, defines a 'good man' as being 'according to the Christian metaphysic . . . the man who worships God because he is united to God in Jesus Christ', and with this we may agree. But it does not lead very far in the undertaking Dr Munby supposes himself to be pursuing—of deducing from the Christian metaphysic a Christian social ethic. Indeed, one thing it leads to in Dr Munby's hands is the assertion that 'the Christian faith provides no clear directives for society . . .', though this is modified by the claim (which seems both vague and subversive) that 'it shows that, for men in society, as individually, being is prior to action, status more important than function, relationships more fundamental than organisations'.[1] If no clear directives are written into the Christian revelation, however, the process by which men are persuaded to accept Dr Munby's desire to applaud a 'widening of the range of human choice' will be much the same as the process by which the 'inquisition or the Kirk Session' make men accept their suspicion of it. It will be by the exercise of authority where authority declares what it takes to be the case and where its power to command comes from the fact that, for a variety of reasons (including sometimes fear), men accept its right to determine what they will take to be the content of God's Law. Dr Munby displays a more than conventional piety in claiming that it is 'not for man to discriminate where God has refused to do so'. In practice men have to, and do, discriminate: and there can be no *philosophical* objection to anyone having practical prejudices different from Dr Munby's. Just as the authority Dr Munby claims in giving social content to Christian principles does not arise from the authority he claims as an explanatory philosopher, so his authority

[1] *Christianity and the Economic Problem*, p. 25.

as a political philosopher is not strengthened by his desire to provide guidance of this sort. And if he is certainly at liberty to assert that, in spite of the benefits it brings, 'the development of a pushing resourceful entrepreneurial class' proclaiming its devotion '"in the name of God and of profit" is not a pleasant sight',[1] it may equally reasonably be asserted that 'few sights are more unpleasant than a scholar who, carefully avoiding the temptation to use his talents to consecrate the existing order of society, uses them instead to consecrate, as the expression of God's Will, one style of criticism of it'.

Those who are aware of these difficulties are not always successful in avoiding them. One may accept Canon Demant's remark that 'we shall not hear God's Word correctly if we identify this or that system with the ultimate will of God' (though, even as an explanatory statement, it is open to the objection that it may be God's Will that we *should* identify 'this system or that' with 'His ultimate Will'). There can, on the other hand, be no doubt about the persuasive character of the apparently explanatory assertion that 'we should be failing to respond to His call to us if we did not commit ourselves to a programme we honestly believed to make the lot of men more tolerable'. Assuming that this is not just a formal statement—that we should do good rather than evil—it is difficult to conceive of a substantive basis for the assertion that we '*ought*' to commit ourselves to a 'programme'. Is it not possible that God's Will may be that we (or some of us, at least) should remain in that condition of political indifference or indecision which precludes commitment to a 'programme'? Why should it be assumed, unless we accept Canon Demant's *authority*, that 'such a commitment is a necessary part of

[1] *God and the Rich Society*, p. 48.

obedience to the divine will'?[1] Why, again, is it to be taken that 'the cultural side of life ... has a precedence over politics and economic activities' or that 'cultural bonds are more essentially spiritual and universal than political or economic ones'?[2] Why is it necessarily wrong for 'Members of Parliament ... to "represent" this or that business interest'? why should not 'success in economic enterprise [be] supposed to be a qualification for rulership'? and how can one be certain that pursuit of economic well-being to the detriment of the 'arts, knowledge and ceremonies' is unnatural?

Canon Demant is in no different case from Mr Philip Mason, who, after explaining the nature of the racial dilemma in Africa, attempts to apply the principles of the New Testament to the practical problems confronting those who govern the continent. That New Testament parables would mean something in Christ's mind cannot be doubted, but exactly *what*, in circumstances which had not then arisen, it is difficult to know. More interpretations than one are possible of the duties of white governments towards their coloured citizens. In relation to South Africa Mr Mason remarks[3] that the government's 'declared principles are contrary to what most Christians would believe morally right', but it is equally clear that some Christians do not share the view he quotes. The Dutch Reformed Church in South Africa does not take this view and it would be unreasonable to dismiss its attitude because it has an interest in the matter. In these circumstances the answer to the question, 'what attitude should an individual or a government take?', will depend as much on answering the question, 'on whose authority should they take it?' as on any specific determination of what it is 'right to

[1] V. A. Demant, *Religion and the Decline of Capitalism* (1952), pp. 177–8.
[2] Demant, p. 184.
[3] P. Mason, *Christianity and Race* (1956), p. 151.

do'. The sentence following the sentence just quoted 'but I do not think one can compromise over the principles', involving a belief that the South African 'government's attack on liberty . . . is wrong by every moral standard'[1] is not an explanatory statement but a powerful persuasion to action. Mr Mason's capacity to inspire assent should vary, not according to his competence as an expository historian or his reputation as a demolisher of second-rate racial science, but according to his authority as a political persuader. Mr Mason, Dr Munby and Canon Demant may certainly, if they feel obliged to, preach a practical political message, and in the case of Canon Demant this must seem doubly appropriate in a teaching priest. Confusion in explanation follows, nevertheless, when injunctions are put in an explanatory form. If one cannot object when writers follow the common practice in doing so, those who maintain explanatory pretensions (as one would expect a Student of Christ Church, a Fellow of Nuffield and, perhaps, even the Director of the Institute of Race Relations to do), ought always to remember that the most innocent assumptions call in explanation for scrutiny and care.

The difficulty in all these cases is to know where to look for resolution of the conflict of opinion by which all practical determination is surrounded. 'Reasoning' will certainly make the choice between the various possible contents which substantive words imply: but it is necessary to be clear what sort of reasoning is possible. If it is taken to be 'reasoning' in an explanatory manner, there is no reason to think it will. Calculation of consequences and consideration of circumstances are important, but they will not effect the transition from the contentless injunction to do good unless prior

---

[1] Mason, p. 152.

commitment is given to one style of political action rather than another. There is, indeed, no other way of deciding in practice between the numerous possibilities that follow from any general injunction than by making to one of them an arbitrary commitment. Nor is there any reason to think that reasons which claim to be 'rational' will necessarily be more effective than persuasions that are justified by any other name.

It is open to Dr Glanville Williams to argue consistently and polemically throughout *The Sanctity of Life and the Criminal Law* against the reluctance of Catholic theologians to condone legal connivance at what they take to be sexual sin. His rhetoric will deepen the convictions held on these questions by those who already share his positions. It would, however, be wrong to expect it to have authority with those who do not. The legality of laws is unaffected by the reasons adduced for enacting them: and there is no need to treat arguments from utility and convenience with greater respect than any others. 'Utility' and 'convenience' are the practical slogans with which Dr Glanville Williams and those who follow him, find their bearings in developing attitudes to political problems: their authority depends on the willingness of citizens to think them worthy of use. In explanation they must be seen to be partial and practical. They, no less than the commitments of catholics defy, to use Dr Williams's words, 'rational enquiry and solution since [they] pertain to metaphysics and emotion and not to empirical facts'. But if, in explanation, it is true, as Dr Williams, in a particular connection, claims, that the 'the pretension of the moral theologian ... must be rejected',[1] so also must the pretension of the enlightened humanist sitting in judgement on him.

Professor Hart, in discussing Sir Patrick Devlin's

---

[1] *Sanctity of Life and the Criminal Law* (1958), p. 282.

The Enforcement of Morals, observes that the 'last distinguished English lawyer [before Sir Patrick] . . . to deliver himself of general reasoned views about the relationship of morality and the criminal law', was Sir F. J. Stephen.[1] One may agree with this, whilst not being clear that interesting 'general reasoning' either gives greater legal authority than the judgements with which less interesting judges have decorated their judicial careers, or that it gives any sort of explanatory authority. Sir Patrick himself claims to be taking further than they intended the 'admirable' attempt the Wolfenden Committee had made (as 'law reformers so rarely do') to 'set out clearly and carefully what in relation to its subjects it considers the function of the law to be',[2] asserts that this is 'of practical importance' because 'a law that appears to be arbitrary and illogical . . . forfeits respect' and proposes to take as his starting-point 'the statements of principle in the Wolfenden Report'. This again is unexceptionable. When Sir Partick goes on, however, to claim that he is 'composing a paper on the jurisprudence of morality', that he is 'concerned only with general principles' and that he does 'not intend to express any opinion one way or another about [practical conclusions]', one is conscious of a certain confusion. What distinguishes his 'general principles' is not that they are not concerned with 'practical conclusions', but that, though concerned solely with practical conclusions, they are so in so general a manner as to lack specific content. Sir Patrick's lecture has not been less effective for this reason: so far as prior commitment led him to 'feel handicapped . . . if [he] thought that [he] was addressing an audience which had no sense of sin or which thought

---

[1] *The Listener*, 30 July 1959, p. 162.
[2] Devlin, *The Enforcement of Morals* (1959), p. 3.

of crime as something quite different', his lecture has given support to those who in principle share this view. Nevertheless, in doing this, he is merely replacing one set of principles—the set which flow from the Wolfenden Committee's assumption that 'it is not, in our view, the function of the law to interfere in the private lives of citizens . . . further than is necessary for the purposes we have outlined'—with another which arises from the assumptions that 'immorality . . . for the purpose of the law, is what every right-minded person is presumed to consider to be immoral', that 'the law must protect . . . the institutions and the community of ideas, political and moral, without which people cannot live together' and that, since 'Christian morals are the basis of the criminal law, . . . without the support of the churches, the moral order, which has its origin in and takes its strength from Christian beliefs, would collapse'.[1]

However, if these are arbitrary commitments (to which 'empirical' evidence is irrelevant), Professor Hart's criticisms display arbitrary commitment also. His opening quotation from John Stuart Mill—that 'the only purpose for which power can be rightfully exercised over any member of a civilised community against his will is to prevent harm to others'[2] has the same persuasive status as the principles enunciated by Sir Patrick and the Wolfenden Committee. To say (not exactly as Sir Patrick does but as Professor Hart makes him) that a 'practice is immoral if the thought of it makes the man on the Clapham omnibus sick' is to imply a preference for a certain style of law and a certain style of morality: but, if Sir Patrick supposes 'the man on the Clapham omnibus' to have what he thinks sensible opinions, the arbitrariness of the assumption is no bar to making other people think so also. Professor Hart is right to question

[1] Devlin, pp. 16, 23–4.   [2] *The Listener*, 30 July 1959, p. 162.

68

Sir Patrick's belief that unless the law does enforce morals, society will collapse (for Sir Patrick's view, no less than his own, supposes that history provides evidence about questions of this sort). But when he opposes to Sir Patrick's preferences the demand that we should summon 'all the resources of our reason, sympathetic understanding [and] critical intelligence' in order to ask whether 'the general morality is based on ignorance, superstition or misunderstanding', there is no reason to accept the implication that Sir Patrick's 'reason, sympathetic understanding and critical intelligence' cannot 'reasonably' reach conclusions about these questions different from his own. Professor Hart (and Sir Patrick for that matter) suppose themselves to be 'reasoning' about moral opinions: but, if they are, their reasoning reaches no decisive conclusion. On the contrary the reasoning itself leads only to the point at which one choice or another has to be made. Moral opinion is changed as often by innuendo as by 'rational' argument. When 'reasonable' is used as a persuasive slogan with unpleasant innuendoes, it is a powerful instrument in forming opinion. To use the word 'reasonable', however, does not ensure that an argument *is* reasonable and much will be gained in explanation by recognizing that this is so.

Finally there is misunderstanding about the nature of political explanation involving a belief that it should supersede the reign of unreflecting prejudice by telling people what their principles suggest they ought to do. Analysis of the common assumptions of political discussion is a primary philosophical task with definite (though unpredictable) results in the world of action. But analysis and explanation are the only philosophical functions, not calculation of consequences or determination of policy. Metaphysical inventiveness, moral altruism and intellectual impartiality provide no necessary basis for authority in practical political conduct. Political decisions are determined by the practical political judgement (which varies according to the character and experience of those who exercise it). Also, they are taken from day to day and hour to hour, sometimes in anger or haste, and often so spontaneously that those who take them do not realize what they have done. This, though it may seem reckless or deplorable, is how decisions have often been taken in the past and it is how they are likely to be taken in the future. The act of decision and the unreflecting choice testify as much to human rationality, or lack of it, and the difficulties of the human condition as any more selfconscious manner: and those who suppose that applied philosophical doctrines can secure a more controlled style of politics are unlikely to act very differently themselves or, when given political responsibility, to be any less at the mercy of accident, interest and miscalculation than any who have gone before them.

Philosophy is explanation not injuction to action, just as history is explanation not justification of the past: and between all sorts of explanatory activity and political practice there is a gap. Unfortunately, this has not always been seen in the last sixty years by those who conduct political studies in English universities: and it is not always seen now. 'A political philosophy', writes Professor Rees, 'is at the same time a political programme.'[1] 'Political Theory', writes Sir Isaiah Berlin, 'is a branch of moral philosophy, which starts from the discovery or application, of moral notions in the sphere of political relations.'[2] 'Social administration', claims

---

[1] J. C. Rees in *Political Studies* (1954), p. 252.
[2] *Two Concepts of Liberty* (1958), p. 5.

Professor Titmuss, 'is concerned ... with the moral values implicit in social action'.[1] 'In the past fifty years', says the Provost of King's, 'political philosophy has been enshrined as one of the most valuable of disciplines in our universities because it is directly concerned with "values".'[2]

As a discipline [states Professor Robson], which seeks to study and to solve the political and governmental problems which confront mankind, [the] importance [of Political Science] cannot be exaggerated. To show the nations how to achieve peace and security: to prevent the fruits of scientific research in the atomic age from destroying civilisation; to find ways of controlling in the general interest the exercise of excessive economic power without stifling industrial initiative or reducing economic efficiency: to reveal methods of governmental action by which the standard of living can be raised, mass unemployment prevented and the trade cycle brought under control: to satisfy the demand for social equality without surrendering the liberties already won or abandoning the struggle for freedoms not yet attained; to discern how political action may enhance the sense of community, stimulate men and women to greater efforts for the common good, and relieve the misery of the oppressed, the underprivileged and the backward peoples, these are the authentic aims of the political scientist no less than the cure of sickness, the reduction of infant and maternal mortality . . . are the proper aims of the medical man.[3]

The obvious places are not the only places from which claims of this sort emerge. Mr David Butler would not criticize Hobbes for being speculative or theoretical if he had not supposed that philosophy could be something else.[4] Part of Dr Gellner's objection to the 'linguistic philosophy' is that it provides 'an activity . . . tailor-made

---

[1] R. M. Titmuss, *Essays on 'The Welfare State'* (1958), p. 14.
[2] Noël Annan, *The Curious Strength of Positivism in English Political Thought* (1959), p. 16.
[3] W. A. Robson, *The University Teaching of Political Science.* U.N.E.S.C.O. (1954), pp. 51–2.
[4] David Butler, *The Study of Political Behaviour*, pp. 27–39.

for the requirements of some of the people who find themselves inheriting the task of teaching philosophy in the universities: a *neutral* realm from which no guidance and no commitment on substantive issues is required'.[1] He, however, might have been more cautious if he had remembered Miss Margaret MacDonald shifting the business of political theory from giving *general*, to giving *specific*, reasons why we *should* obey or disobey the State[2] or if he had examined the implication of Mr Hare's claim that 'our present generation is . . . painfully trying to become morally adult by . . . learning to make decisions of principle; to learn to use "ought"-sentences in the realization that they can only be verified by reference to a standard or set of principles which we have by our own decision accepted and made our own'.[3]

When Professor Hart, after rejecting the view that 'certain rules cannot be law because of their moral iniquity', announces a preference for the utilitarian view that 'laws may be law but too evil to be obeyed', he has said something of importance. This, however, does not mean that we have to follow him when he claims that 'perhaps the most important single lesson to be learned from this form of the denial of the Utilitarian distinction is the one that the utilitarians were most concerned to teach: when we have the ample resources of plain speech, we must not present the moral criticism of institutions as propositions of a disputable philosophy'.[4] What *practical* reason makes it so important that the West German court (which he criticizes in the preceding pages) should not misuse the 'propositions of natural law philosophy' if it wants to? Concern

[1] E. Gellner, *Words and Things* (1959), p. 153.
[2] Margaret MacDonald, 'The Language of Political Theory' in A. G. N. Flew, *Logic and Language* (1955), pp. 177–8.
[3] R. M. Hare, *The Language of Morals* (1952), pp. 77–8.
[4] *71 Harvard Law Review*, pp. 620–1, but cf. Hart, *Concept of Law*, pp. 254–5.

for the integrity of philosophical words in philosophical discourse provides no reason why others should not use them for their own purposes elsewhere. The history of morals does not, as Professor Hart supposes, teach that 'the only thing to do with a moral quandary is not to hide it'.[1] The history of morals teaches no lessons: and there is no reason for the philosopher to be concerned when in practice he sees statements of his own used for purposes to which he would not himself professionally want to put them.

Nor does Professor Northcote Parkinson, who has the reputation of a reactionary wit, fail in high seriousness either. 'There would seem to be no fundamental reason', he writes in the concluding pages of *The Evolution of Political Thought*, 'why there should not be as fresh a departure in politics as there has been in physics. . . . When, if ever, research leads to definite conclusions, when, if ever, states prove sufficiently enlightened to accept advice based on patient investigation rather than on crude emotion and selfish interest, mankind may break away from the treadmill which seems to lead from kingship to democracy, from democracy to kingship.' And even if it is by no means certain that they will, 'we may still be assured that the principles we seek, which we know to be neither universal nor eternal, will never be discovered except by scientific means. When found, our rules will have only a restricted validity. But without curiosity, without method, they will never be found at all.'[2]

That these confusions exist is a pity. Each activity has its limits and there is no discredit in confining pretensions to the limits of the activity itself. The limit of academic explanation is that it explains the subject-matter and

[1] 71 *Harvard Law Review*, p. 620.
[2] C. N. Parkinson, *The Evolution of Political Thought* (1958), pp. 314, 316.

nothing else. Other things (styles of political action, for example) may occur in consequence: but when they give advice about the conduct of political practice, political philosophers have no necessary authority; no more than as citizens, and much less than those who have responsibility for action.

Professor Macrae[1] claims that 'one becomes a sociologist' 'because one wants not only to understand but also to change society' but fails to realize that the objection to this is not to the fact of wanting to *change* society but to the concern with wanting to do anything to society at all. It is not so much *change* which offends (for a desire to use an academic subject to preserve the existing order would be as irrelevant) but that anyone should put in the forefront of his academic concern a preoccupation with improving purposes. If 'sociologists *are* very liable to find things out about society that call for reform',[2] 'calling for reform' is not an activity in which they have professional authority. It ought therefore not to be their *first* preoccupation and, if it is, it lessens the probability that their work will achieve explanatory usefulness. In what way is it relevant for Professor Macrae, in an otherwise illuminating discussion of Professor Talmon's writing, to complain that 'the danger ... is that it may reinforce a tendency in the West to idolise our present and transient relations and institutions'?[3] Professor Talmon in fact is concerned about the practical consequences of his writing: but is his concern an academic one? Is it an academic criticism of his history that it tends in a 'most unfortunate direction'? No doubt in practice 'we must not turn an idolatry of the present into a domestic system of thought control': but nothing would more closely

[1] D. G. Macrae, *Ideology and Society* (1961), p. 178.
[2] Macrae, p. 4.   [3] Macrae, p. 221.

resemble an academic system of thought-control than the feeling that a relevant criticism of the tendency of a work of historical explanation is that it will produce unfortunate political results in future. Professor Macrae's volume of essays is liberally sprinkled with arbitrarinesses of this sort. Is there 'nothing more important' in existing society 'than to know where society is going':[1] if there has, of late, been a great increase in the 'most powerful enemy of reason in the western world ... suspicion and conformity', is that any reason for thinking that social science is more necessary than it would be otherwise?[2] Are 'all rational arguments of fact and advantage in favour of tolerance'?[3] And is there not a serious limitation in the failure to see that the word 'reason', so far from presenting in explanatory writing the opportunity to enunciate such pious incantations as that 'social scientists ... are animated by the hope born 250 years ago of finding, by the paths of reason, some Avilion of reason and justice', demands in reality explanation of the fact that the content Professor Macrae imputes to 'reason' is not the content imputed by everyone else?

Again, we may agree when Lord Robbins dissociates himself from the claim that 'Economics should not only take account of valuations and ethical standards ... but that also it should pronounce upon the ultimate validity of these valuations and standards'.[4] It is, however, not possible to agree with his reason—that whilst 'economics deals with ascertainable facts: ethics deals with valuations and obligations'.[5] Although ethical philosophers certainly do deal with 'valuations and obligations', they should show towards them the same attitude as economists should show towards theirs; an explanatory

[1] Macrae, p. 86.   [2] Macrae, p. 59.   [3] Macrae, p. 105.
[4] Lionel Robbins, *The Nature and Significance of Economic Science* (1935), p. 147.
[5] Robbins, p. 148.

attitude which takes as the subject-matter the fact that men make valuations and feel obligations, and attempts to explain what it is they are doing when they do so. Not only the economist, but also the ethical philosopher, should give to the subject-matter with which he is concerned the sort of attention which will make the several practical activities—of producing and distribuing goods on the one hand, of making moral judgements on the other—intelligible to explanatory enquiry. It is not, as Lord Robbins supposes, because 'Ethics' determines the ends and 'Economics' the means, that Ethics is separate from Economics: but that the subject-matter requiring attention in Ethics is not coterminous with the subject-matter requiring attention in Economics.

A similar mistake is made by Professor Marshall who, in disclaiming for the sociologist responsibility for determining the choice of *ends*, claims that 'every honest sociologist, like every honest economist, knows that the choice of ends or ideals lies outside the field of social science and within the field of social philosophy'.[1] He is right in one respect (that it lies outside the field of social science) but wrong in the assumption that, since the choice of ends is not the function of social science, therefore it must be a function of social 'philosophy'. 'Social philosophy' is an explanatory activity and has functions suitable to a lecture-room. Just as 'economics' is the attempt to make economic activity intelligible, so 'social science' and 'social philosophy' should be the attempt to make intelligible the body of political activity whose existence constitutes the subject-matter requiring explanation and one part of which is choosing of 'ends' in economic and social action. 'Social philosophy' is not the activity of choosing ends.

[1] *Citizenship and Social Class* (1950), pp. 2–3.

'Social philosophy' is reflection upon the fact that ends are constantly being chosen in practice—reflection which leads to explanation; and to nothing else.

Often the claims made for the practical relevance of the subject are cautiously expressed: but that does not make them less objectionable. There is no reason to agree with Dr Ewing that 'some training in ethical and political philosophy is likely to enable one to help more efficiently in deciding ethical and political questions that arise in practice'.[1] There is no need to accept that position, and it is right to accuse him of illegitimately annexing the practical political 'reason' to philosophical explanation when he claims that, although 'neither good will without thought, nor intuition, nor inductive generalisation, nor reasoning is by itself adequate for ethical and political practice ... the philosopher should be specially qualified to make suggestions about the fourth factor required, reasoning'.[2] If, as he admits, 'conclusions in political philosophy can never be as definite as one would like, because they are made to some extent in abstraction' and if 'the philosopher cannot *prove* what ought to be done', then there can be no reason to conclude that '[the philosopher] may still be employed usefully when dealing with particular concrete situations'.[3] Dr Ewing is arguing here that whilst 'general ethical reasoning cannot by itself *prove*, it may *help* us to see that an action is right or wrong'; and gives as a reason for this the fact that, whilst the question 'what laws the politician should introduce to help a particular state cannot be adequately decided by the philosopher as such', this can only be decided 'by a person with *expert* [my italics] knowledge of the relevant empirical facts'. The objection to both

[1] A. C. Ewing, *The Individual, The State and World Government* (1947), p. 7.
[2] Ewing, p. 7.   [3] Ewing, p. 4.

77

these positions is considerable. The first statement is, in a formal sense, adequate: 'general ethical reasoning ... may help us to see ...': but there is no reason to suppose that 'general ethical reasoning' is most competently or authoritatively carried on by philosophers. On the contrary, if by 'general ethical reasoning' is meant reasoning with a view to action, then it is conducted with adequate competence by all citizens at varying levels of articulation. Every society has a general stock of ideas, many of which are no doubt inconsistent with one another, but none of which needs the competence of the philosopher in order to be enunciated adequately. Philosophers *can* help to clarify an ethical disposition: but it is no necessary part of their work to do so. Nor is the assumption implicit in the second statement more satisfactory than the first. If it is true that philosophers cannot claim to decide what laws a state should have, they have no greater claim to determine in what direction they should *tend*. As citizens, of course, they will: but, if Dr Ewing excludes the more detailed determination from the professional purview, is there any reason to include the vaguer one? And is it anything but a summary of the misconceptions with which we are dealing to claim that, 'the war won, what is required to end the nightmare of wars, wars from which we periodically suffer, is not a heroic sacrifice nor a supremely ingenious piece of political machinery, but *merely* [my italics] the guidance of our political actions by reason (or common sense, if you like to put it that way) so far as to apply consistently to states those ethical principles which are generally recognised as applying to individuals'.[1]

Where Dr Ewing makes explicit the assumptions against which we are arguing, others make them by

[1] Ewing, p. 317.

78

implication, often almost, it seems, inadvertently. When Professor Oakeshott says that political activity takes 'the form because it can take no other [of] amendment of existing arrangements by exploring and pursuing what is intimated in them', he is making a powerful, explanatory observation. When, however, he goes on, uncharacteristically, to claim that 'our mistakes will be less frequent and less disastrous . . . if we escape the illusion that politics can ever be anything more than the pursuit of intimations',[1] he is imputing to sensible, explanatory language practical consequences which there is no reason to think it will produce. If those who pursue coherent explanation also maintain the prejudice of hoping that successful explanation may lead to improvement of political conduct, that is one thing: but there is no reason to suppose that sensible explanation will have sensible consequences in practice, or that the tradition which supposes that its chief function is to provide guidance for action will *necessarily* in action be more disastrous than any other. Its claim as explanation may well be ridiculous: but there is no reason to suppose that those who use this sort of language may not play a perfectly recognizable part in political practice. Lord Stansgate's assertion that the judicial judgement in the Bristol Election Case showed that 'Bristol South-East electors, for trying to challenge the hereditary system with their votes must be punished by having a man they rejected' is, by any explanatory standard, nonsense. It may be reasonable to assert that the law in England is such that the judges' decision 'reveals for all to see the fundamentally undemocratic nature of the law as they see it', (*Manchester Guardian*, 29 July, 1961), but that is another matter. Nevertheless, however absurd Lord Stansgate's

[1] M. J. Oakeshott, *Political Education* (1951), p. 19–20.

statement may be in explanation, the acclamation with which it was received is evidence of its practical utility in reminding a public which is not deeply interested in Lord Stansgate's future of the objection he feels to his own involuntary ennoblement.

We may, again, take it that Professor Oakeshott's review[1] of Lord Hailsham's *The Case for Conservatism* was an attempt to support the view that Lord Hailsham's 'principles' have no explanatory standing, and with this we may agree. But we may not agree with what is taken to follow. It does not follow, because Lord Hailsham's 'principles' have no philosophical standing, that he should not want to display them. It is legitimate to warn an academic audience that Lord Hailsham is not, in this context, an academic person (any more than Professors Cole and Laski were in so many of theirs). But it is outside the range of academic competence to suggest that work of this sort has no value. The outpouring of higher Conservative propaganda between 1945 and 1950 may, as a matter of practical political calculation, not have been necessary to victory at the election of 1951: but those who managed the Conservative Party thought it was. They hoped to remove the impression, which they thought important at the election of 1945, that no reasoning person could vote Conservative, and to kill the myth that the Labour Party had a monopoly of academic intelligence. *The Case for Conservatism*, by an ex-Fellow of All Souls, was a contribution to this task. Professor Oakeshott feared that Lord Hailsham wished merely to replace a Socialist set of pseudo-philosophical principles with a Conservative set, and would, therefore, no less than socialist propagandists themselves, hinder the effort to see political activity as it really is. It was reasonable for Professor

[1] *Cambridge Journal*, vol. i, pp. 474 ff.

Oakeshott, as a citizen, to dislike this; it was necessary for him as a philosopher to give warning against allowing that sort of work to infiltrate into academic writing: but it is no more legitimate to imply that Professor Oakeshott had high authority in performing the practical function than it is to suppose that Lord Hailsham had authority to perform the academic one.

Professor Oakeshott is aware of this difficulty. His general position (sketched in *Political Education* and the Preface to *Hobbes's Leviathan* and implied in *Experience and its Modes*) leaves a willing reader in no doubt. Nor need one ignore the fact that the academic situation in 1948 (to say nothing of the political one), may have called for assertions of this sort. Then, as now, supporters of the liberal orthodoxy in political studies assumed, not just that their assumptions were valid in practice, but that they had academic authority also. Then, as now, it was a necessary part of the academic dialectic to show that academic competence could be geared to support positions contrary to the prevailing wind. All that is needed to complete the explanatory process is to carry the dialectic to the point of establishing that not only has the prevailing liberalism no authority, but that neither Mr Weldon's emotionless practical judgement nor Professor Oakeshott's consultation of the tradition of behaviour (except so far as that is a description of what cannot be avoided), nor any other of the practical slogans with which the most articulate sort of citizen, and most polished sort of politician, console and advance themselves in practice, have any authority in explanation.

Mr Weldon, in general, rejected the belief that political philosophy was capable of providing commands to action. He seemed, nevertheless, to fall victim to it when he ended *The Vocabulary of Politics* with the words 'what we need to get us out of our political difficulties is a good deal more thought and a good deal less emotion'[1] and when, in rejecting the demand that philosophers should support a subjectivism of principle,[2] he points out that 'quite ordinary people do succeed in using significantly all the appraisal words and statements', that '[they] do not think that when they do so they are just reporting their personal references' and that 'they produce reasons in supporting these statements'. They do this, he suggests, because 'they avoid the intellectualist error of pretending that there must be one test . . . of a single metrical type which will finally settle or provide objective answers to all proper questions'.

In fact, of course, 'quite ordinary people . . . succeed in using significantly . . . appraisal words' not because they are thoughtful, detached and uncommitted but because they, no less than the 'victims of the intellectualist error', simplify, dogmatize and rigidify the authority of the 'principles' to which in practice they attach as much significance as anyone more articulate to the principles he happens to follow. Nor does the fact that 'quite ordinary people' do not think they are 'just reporting their personal preferences' mean that the philosopher has to accept the evaluation they make of the function their reasoning fulfils. It is unlikely that most people would in practice long defend decisions, choices or preferences they thought 'unreasonable' or that they might not, if pressed and articulate, be able to give 'reasons' for making them; but that would not mean that the 'reasonable' argument they would offer would avoid unargued, arbitrary commitment. The objection to Mr Weldon here is partly that he ignores the intensity of commitment shown by 'quite ordinary

<hr>

[1] Weldon, *Vocabulary of Politics* (1953), p. 193.   [2] Weldon, p. 150.

people', partly that he seems for a moment unwilling to recognize that the 'radical intellectualism' he is attacking is inappropriate to philosophy not because it has no relevance to practice but because, as he well knew, its tendency to be obsessed by the task of providing clear, determinate practical principles is not philosophy at all. Nor does the 'subjectivism' which he disavows[1] deserve the censure he gives it. Here he confuses 'subjectivism' in political practice with the philosophical style of thinking that is called 'subjectivism'. If people want to argue 'well, we do things in this way here and now, but people do them differently at other places and times . . . and you may please yourself', that is an attitude in political practice whose exponents may well, as he suggests, succumb to those who are more certain of the rightness of their positions. It is, however, not one which the philosopher has authority to criticize or condemn. It is very different from the philosophical doctrine called 'subjectivism'—which assumes that, whatever certainties men may in practice have, the philosopher cannot by *philosophical* reasoning give them necessary content. Since the philosopher should be concerned to explore the implications of the fact that opinions vary about the content of practical certainties, it is irrelevant in a work like Mr Weldon's to suggest either that 'more thought' instead of 'less emotion' will get us out of our practical difficulties (is there, in any case, any practical reason to think it will?) or that it is (on Mr Weldon's assumptions and ours) the philosopher's business to try to make it do so. The fact is that, alongside a clear commitment to the position that the function of 'philosophical thought' is to get us out of our *philosophical* difficulties, and in spite of explicit assertions to the contrary, there remained, even in Mr Weldon,

---

[1] Weldon, p. 147.

traces of an emotional assumption (left over from *States and Morals*), that, if only thought were clearer, if only metaphysical political lumber were cleared away and if only the assumptions of his own style of philosophy were applied to political practice in order to expose the absurdities of democratic, Hegelian or Marxist theory, political activity might be conducted less emotionally and more sanely, and 'many of our political difficulties avoided'.

This also is why Bradley's *My Station and Its Duties* is untransparently conservative at a crucial point. In discussing the view that 'Conscience . . . wants you to have no law but yourself, and to be better than the world' and that 'to wish to be better than the world is to be already on the threshold of immorality',[1] he observes, rightly, that the '"the world" in this sense . . . is the morality already existing ready to hand in laws, institutions, social usages, moral opinions and feelings', that not only has it 'given moral content [to the young but] is the only source of such content'.[2] One may accept the view, also, that 'it is . . . a duty, standing on the basis of the existing, and in harmony with its general spirit, to try and make not only oneself but also the world better, or rather, and in preference, one's own world better'. But when he goes on to suggest that 'it is another thing, starting from oneself, from ideals in one's head, to set oneself and them against the moral world', it is difficult to follow. 'The moral world', he claims, 'with its social institutions is a fact: it is real: our "ideals" are not real . . . we should learn to see the great moral fact in the world . . . actual existence'.[3] This, however, does not grasp the important point about the nature of 'ideals'. It is true that they are, as

[1] *Ethical Studies* (ed. 1927), p. 199.
[2] *Ethical Studies* (ed. 1927), pp. 199–200.
[3] *Ethical Studies* (ed. 1927), p. 200.

84

Bradley says, 'abstractions', but abstractions from what? It cannot always be claimed that they are abstractions from the moral history of the society of which they are a part: but this often *can* be claimed. It often is not claimed in these words because the reformer has a preference for the language of conscience instead. Exaggerated use of the language of conscience is as offensive to the present writer as it was to Bradley: but its function has still to be understood. Even when reformers 'set themselves' against the world of existing morality, it is likely that the abstraction they are pursuing will be a crude summary of the moral intimations of the society in which they have been reared—an abridgement of an abridgement of part of its practice. Even if abridgement of this sort provides no explanation of the nature of a society's moral practice, it does not follow that it is useless. Certainly it is easy to forget that, just as 'moral principles' are an abridgement of practice in the past, so, since the circumstances have not yet arisen, they supply only an abridged injunction to action in the future. Certainly abridgement, when used as a guide to action, will neither resolve the difficulties which moral activity involves nor guarantee the control at which it aims. Certainly reformers are absurd who, failing to see that they justify action by reference to an abridgement of practice rather than by reference to practice itself, suppose that it will. Nevertheless, since those who claim to follow the moral practice of society are able, no more than the conscientious rebel, to grasp its history in concrete diversity, they are usually guided by abridgement also. It is true that there are cases in which men do not feel *compelled* to justify their decisions: and that there *are* men who seldom justify them at all: but about them it is unnecessary to speak. It is true further that, once a point of precision is reached in the

85

act of justification, consideration of circumstances may play so large a part that the principles gain concrete identity. It is true, also, that those who use the language of 'conformity to the practice of society', when confronted with the need to make specific choices, will not always justify their choices in the language of principle. But this does not alter the fact that they, no less than the followers of conscience, have principles: and that the followers of conscience, no less than they, do in practice judge practically and choose pragmatically, however self-righteous the language in which they justify their decisions.

If this is so, however, can it be taken that Bradley's explanatory statements show in this connection anything more than arbitrary prejudice directed, not at the function performed by reformers, but at the language in which they clothe, the rhetoric with which they dignify, and the self-righteousness with which they surround the function they perform? The language of conscience is indeed absurd, and it is agreeable, and characteristic, to find Bradley moved by so healthy a distaste. But, if the object is to subject moral reformers to *philosophical* curtailment, it is useless merely to replace one way of justifying one's preferences with another. All *philosophy* can do, but what it most certainly *ought* to do, is to explain that the claims made by those who use this sort of language have no philosophical authority (though they have what practical authority they can muster). Since no philosophical reason can support the claims which the language of conscience almost always implies, the affectation of superiority is a practical tactic which there is no obligation to meet in philosophical terms. Those who dislike this language need feel no 'philosophical' embarrassment at answering, not in the dignified language of the 'science of ethics', but in the earthier language of practical prejudice. All intimations of this sort—whether to 'obey' or to 'set oneself against the moral world'—have, philosophically, a similar status. The claim that one of them is philosophically superior is mistaken, and if men do in practice take seriously the assertion that decisions of conscience have logical, philosophical or academic authority, philosophy may free them of inhibitions they suffer on that account. To go further, however, is to express preferences in moral practice; and, in this particular context, Bradley, like Professor Oakeshott—and in the same good cause— goes a good deal further than he should. Nowhere, in spite of Bradley's criticisms of this chapter, in the half-chapter following, is one more powerfully reminded of the complaint of Graham Wallas that when 'Mr Chesterton cries out ... against those who complicate the life of man, and tells us to eat "caviare on impulse" instead of "grapenuts on principle" [he is], since we cannot unlearn our knowledge ... only telling us to eat caviare on principle':[1] though it is right to add that no one knew better than Chesterton that the best way to expose the arbitrariness of the principles of the high-minded was, whether having any serious commitment to them or not, provocatively to flaunt an opposite set.

Mr Bambrough, whose general position on these matters is not unacceptable, argues that since 'in all disputes about the value of particular political analogies, the issue is liable to be not only theoretical (logical) but also practical (political) in character, and [since] the task of the logician is to elucidate and to evaluate the arguments that may be urged on both sides, and not to take up the position of one side against the other ... part of this task of elucidation will consist in showing which concrete political proposals are *logically* related to the

[1] *Human Nature in Politics* (1910), p. 183.

acceptance or rejection of particular metaphorical and analogical ways of speaking about politics and politicians'.[1] In what way 'concrete political proposals are *logically* related to the acceptance or rejection of particular metaphorical and analogical ways of speaking about politics and politicians' is, however, far from clear. Presumably it means that logic may point out that the adoption of a political analogy involves wanting particular political actions to be performed because, unless these actions are performed, it is unlikely that the sort of political arrangements implied in the analogy will be brought about. That this is Mr Bambrough's meaning may seem to be confirmed by a letter he wrote in defence of this article.[2] In this he observed that '[political philosophy] could not be less of a merely academic study than it is at the present time, when two such important and otherwise dissimilar authorities as the Vatican and the Kremlin subscribe to the same false view of the nature of political questions and answers, the view that in any political conflict at least one side must be either ignorant or wicked or both and, what is more, demonstrably ignorant or wicked'; and he added not only that 'the faulty logic on which this view is based needs to be corrected if it is not to continue to have undesirable practical consequences' but also that 'those of us who do [this academic] kind of work . . . are indeed defending a traditionally English view of the rights of the individual and the freedom of personal choice and judgement'.

There are about this position at least two difficulties. It is, in the first place, difficult even roughly to know what the general consequences of specific political actions are likely to be. If the question under discussion were

[1] Renford Bambrough in Laslett, *Philosophy, Politics and Society* (1956), p. 103.
[2] *Encounter*, October 1956.

whether purchase tax should be raised by 10 per cent in the next budget, there would be a measure of agreement about the immediate economic consequences. That would be a relatively simple prediction, not necessarily related to a general conception of the nature of a desirable society. If, with Plato and Mr Bambrough, we take *democratic* to mean a polity where no one group has a monopoly of the *techné* of politics and if the question under consideration were: would the raising of purchase tax by 10 per cent help to make Britain a more democratic country?, then the usefulness of the question is not, to say the least, self-evident. If it were answered that the level of purchase tax would not make much difference to 'democracy' anyway, then one may wonder whether proposals which seem to flow more obviously from the injunction behind the democratic analogy are likely to be very much more help either. Could proposals to eliminate inherited wealth or abolish the public schools be 'logically' related to the desire to make Britain more democratic? Specific proposals of this sort have often been justified on this ground: but can one say that they would produce a society more closely resembling the society implied in the analogy? Would it not be plausible to argue that adoption of these policies would produce a ruling class, harder, rougher, more ruthless and less 'democratic' than the ruling class produced by existing arrangements: and that, since neither the one consequence nor the other can be seriously predicted and since neither can be *known* to follow from the proposal under consideration, one is faced with such uncertain possibilities that it is idle to talk of *logically* relating the concrete proposals to the analogy at all. Would it have been *logically* necessary in 1830 to deduce from the platonic (anti-democratic) analogy the conclusion that the proposals embodied in the Reform Bill of 1832 were unacceptable? The statesmen who ruled England in 1890 after sixty years of 'reformed government' were not, as it turned out, markedly different in social origin from those who ruled in 1830. Were Whigs *logically* absurd in arguing to one conclusion and Tories *logically* absurd in arguing to another, from aristocratic assumptions very much the same as those of each other and very much the same as Plato's? It may be argued that Mr Bambrough's statement stands if it is made in a form as general as that 'if we do believe that politics is a *techné*, then we shall believe that a very few men ought always to exercise political power': but so general a statement leaves open so many questions of content that it does not advance further than the analogy itself—particularly when a few men always have in the past exercised the greater part of the political power in any society that has ever existed. The fact is that, if an analogy is general enough to amount to anything more than a set of limited proposals, it is probably impossible to predict that its objectives will be advanced by any particular set of proposals: and if, on the other hand, it is limited enough to be a set of specific proposals itself, then no analogy or metaphor is present. Naturally, if philosophy is to make as transparent as possible the assumptions on which men act, attention must be turned to the nature of the assumptions. It is necessary, also, if adequate explanation is to be given, that incoherencies should be exposed. It is, however, one thing to expose incoherencies and quite another to suppose that the object in exposing them should be to effect any particular consequences more extensive than the consequence of improving the quality of explanatory writing. The Kremlin and the Vatican (no less than Whitehall and Washington) may do otherwise, may, indeed, misuse the conclusions reached in the sort of explanation which scholars ought to give. The sort of philosophy we are advocating may battle against pseudo-philosophies when they are, as a matter of practice, propagated by the Vatican, the Kremlin, Washington, and Whitehall. But, if it should certainly do this, it should do so only in order to explain that their 'self-evident truths' and 'fundamental principles' are guides to action, not aids to explanation. The fact that they are not philosophy, even when coupled with the fact that those who enunciate them think they are, says nothing whatever, and should in explanation be seen to say nothing whatever, about their function in political action. Even if the 'Vatican and the Kremlin' believe, as Mr Bambrough says, that 'at least one side must be ... demonstrably wicked', the control they have over events is no different from the control they would have if, with Mr Bambrough, they believed the opposite. Consequences are not within the control of philosophers (even established ones): and if the Kremlin or Vatican do in fact claim to be giving explanatory accounts of the nature of political obligation, the only thing philosophy needs to do is to explain that their assumptions are inadequate to describe the phenomenon under discussion. There is no need to suggest that one explanation (when taken, as Mr Bambrough wants his taken, as a starting-point for practice) is likely to have practical consequences directly related to its nature: and it is unnecessary in explanation (however desirable in *Encounter*) to buttress an explanatory assumption with references to our 'English' inheritance. Whatever Mr Bambrough, the Pope or the Kremlin's philosophers may say about the connection between theory and practice will affect practice: but the effect will be so devious and unpredictable, and will in any case be so much a matter of practice itself, that nothing will be gained philosophically by arguing from the consequences to the desirability of a certain style of explanation or from a certain style of explanation to the probability of the consequences.

Another example of Mr Bambrough's misconception is provided by Dr A. Victor Murray when he writes[1] that 'the future rests with neither type of authoritarianism, Catholic or Communist. Ideologies which are passionately attached to logical completeness must in the long run be defeated by human nature. It is a characteristic of the problems of human life and destiny that we cannot know all the answers, and any institution which claims otherwise is very rightly suspect.' It is not, at first sight, clear whether this is to be taken as an explanatory statement or as a persuasive one. That it is in fact the latter may be deduced from the claim that 'in such circumstances Protestantism and democracy find themselves to be natural allies', that 'the real evil alike of Roman Catholicism and of Communism is that each is judge in its own cause' and that 'it is of the essence of Protestantism that it takes an entirely different line'.[2] 'The weakness of Protestantism—which is also the weakness of democracy' is said to lie in the fact that 'depending as it does on persuasion and not force, it is characterised by suspense of judgement, not because of lack of conviction but in order to be sure that it can count on the convictions of a sufficient number of people'. Nevertheless, this 'refusal to be judge in its own cause' —'part of the cross which lies heavy on such progressive movements'—is in the long run supposed to be a source of strength. This, indeed, is persuasive writing, designed to suggest to the converted, and convertible, that Protestantism is a thoughtful religion suitable to

[1] A. V. Murray, *The State and the Church in a Free Society* (1958), p. x.
[2] Murray, p. xi.

men who value their independence, make up their own minds and reject the dogmas of authority.

If this is so, however, what are we to make of the claim that 'ideologies which are passionately attached to logical completeness must in the long run be defeated by human nature'. If this is a persuasive statement, it does not *have* to be justified empirically; justification could be allowed to rest on the fact that Dr Murray, speaking as one who has a measure of religious authority, claims to know what human nature requires. In explanation it is not obviously plausible to say that 'human nature' does defeat ideologies of this sort. It can at least as plausibly be argued that men require such ideologies in order, for practical purposes, to know what the world is like and what their duties are within it. If, however, Dr Murray's statement is a persuasive one, it does not differ very obviously in manner from the claims made by the Catholic Church or the Communist Party to provide certain *practical* knowledge of the character of the world and the nature of Man. The reluctance of Dr Murray, and other sophisticated protestants, to admit that a logically complete ideology can provide practical certainty must itself be seen as the manifestation of an 'ideology passionately attached to logical completeness' —with the descriptive proviso that this ideology has as its validating principle the belief that truth and duty can be discerned, not on the authority of the Pope and the Councils or of Marx, Lenin and Mr Khrushchev, but by an alliance between the judgement of the Bible, the Church and the individual conscience. There can be no philosophical objection to Dr Murray using his sort of persuasion and denigration in order to make men protestants: but it is desirable to understand that statements suitable for recommending religious preferences may well lack the transparency necessary to explanation; and that between one persuasive statement (from Dr Murray) and another (from the Pope or Mr Khrushchev), it may be difficult, whatever other differences may be discerned, to discern a logical or existential one.

It is, of course, not just openly religious dogma which masquerades as explanatory truth in order to accumulate authority: those who reject these dogmas engage in a similar masquerade also. Lady Wootton's *Testament for Social Science* is littered with examples. If Lady Wootton were affecting merely to advocate a practical dogma—the dogma of 'Scientific Scepticism' —there could be no objection to her belief that 'my argument ... cannot be acceptable either to the Churches or to the Communists'.[1] Obviously her doctrines are not the doctrines of any of the Christian churches, or of Russian Marxism either. Unfortunately, the reasons she gives for thinking them unacceptable reveal a good deal of confusion. Lady Wootton makes much of the '*scientific* attitude which is really the common foe of both dogmas'[2] but seems not to consider the possibility that the 'scientific attitude', as she uses the phrase, rests on dogma also. It is easy for their enemies to say that 'neither the Communists nor the Church can face with equanimity the attitude which is prepared to follow the argument whithersoever it may lead: likewise neither can tolerate the rival dogma promulgated by the other':[3] but one may reasonably ask whether the 'scientific attitude' does not proselytize also. Can anyone 'follow the argument *whithersoever* it may lead'? and would anyone who did ever be able to adopt any practical attitude to anything? Towards the end of *Social Science and Social Pathology* the same sort of confusion

[1] Barbara Wootton, *Testament for Social Science*, p. 188.
[2] Wootton, p. 189. [3] Wootton, p. 188.

is apparent. After quoting some of the absurder claims made by Dr Stafford-Clark and others on behalf of the normative authority of psychiatry in relation to legal treatment of crime—claims of which Lady Wootton is sceptical—she adds that 'it is clear that medicine is ousting morality in two quarters simultaneously . . . moral judgements are beginning to be excluded from what has hitherto been the area of their most unchallengeable rule: while, on the other hand, with the invention of what has been aptly called "mental healthmanship" medicine takes upon itself the business of defining the Good Life'. This slightly misses the point. What is happening in fact is not that *medicine* is ousting *morality*: but that one morality, whose applications are determined on the authority of lawyers and legislators is being challenged by the authority of doctors whose claims rest, like all other claims to moral authority, on the willingness of those who legislate or make any other sort of authoritative judgement, to accept them. Those who urge that the first thing to do with criminals is to cure them and who argue that determination of the period of 'cure' must be made by medical specialists rather than judges have no *scientific* authority to do so. Dr Stafford-Clark's views about the political question are no more 'scientific' than anyone else's. They are political statements which can be rejected as soon, and as often, as those who have political authority, and maintain contrary persuasions, choose to.

Nor are Lady Wootton's confusions confined to moral and religious questions. It is unlikely that she would 'regret the prevalence of pre-scientific mental habits' and an absence of 'the canons of good empirical reasoning . . . in everyday discussion of public affairs'[1] if she had not supposed that the insights of her particular

---

[1] *Testament*, pp. 48-9.

descriptive expertize provided better guides to political practice than the insights of those who do not happen to have been trained as sociologists. When she complains of the 'practice of ignoring the elementary principles of sampling' and adduces as being amongst the 'grosser deficiencies of this kind ... generalisations about the behaviour, opinions or conditions of foreign people based on the casual contacts of a tourist',[1] she is saying something of consequence in explanation: but she is wrong if she imagines that it is necessarily more 'rational' or 'right' that the prejudices of citizens who feel no urge to count heads should be superseded by the conclusions of sociological investigators. Practice is riddled with confused half-truths: but is not always less adequately accomplished for that reason. Nor is there anything but philosophical confusion (unless it be sociological arrogance) in the claim that although 'parliamentary government with all its imperfections is the best means that we (sic) have been able to devise for combining tolerably efficient government with reasonable freedom for the governed ... I have little doubt that in the long run research in the social sciences' (not, it may be noted, the practice of politicians) 'will suggest much more satisfactory ways of achieving that combination than the (as they will eventually appear) crude instruments which we have so far evolved ... '.[2] Lady Wootton, having given an adequate account of the way in which scientific hypotheses are adumbrated, in the social as well as in the natural sciences, shows no understanding of the limitations from which all science suffers equally, shows no grasp of the fact that the function of a science is to explain to those who want explanation and nothing more; and gives herself unnecessary worry, first by implying that statements in political practice ought

[1] *Testament*, p. 51.   [2] *Testament*, p. 57.

96

to explain (and not persuade) and then by condemning them for failing to do what they are not designed for in the first place. It *is* innocent: but it is not just innocence which leads her to suggest that, if the Labour and Conservative candidates for the local councils whose addresses she has before her and who are 'both . . . emphatic about the vigour with which, if elected, they will build houses and schools', 'equally mean what they say, there could be no reason why they should be fighting one another'. The struggle for power which moves many politicians (and many other people besides) is not a facet of 'pre-scientific' habits only. The dominance of the 'social scientist' would not establish so wide a measure of agreement about political objectives that temperaments would cease to conflict and opinions to be contested. No-one really does make the 'assumption', said to be the one on which two-party arrangements are based, 'that two misrepresentations add up to one true representation'.[1] It is widely understood that the two-party system is a way of choosing governments which happens to have emerged over the last twenty-five years, partly by accident and partly because many people (including politicians) have invested considerable capital in it. Is it not the merest irrelevancy to ask whether 'a two party political system . . . or indeed any party system at all as at present practised is conducive to scientific habits of mind'?[2] Cabinets make the best decisions they can in the light of the circumstances that seem relevant: consideration of circumstances involves judging what they can get away with: and any system which did not operate through party would face roughly the same difficulties as one that does. Explanation requires understanding of the activity under discussion: and one may ask whether it shows any

[1] *Testament*, p. 57. [2] *Testament*, p. 58.

97

understanding of the nature of public political discussion—as conducted by newspapers or by political parties—to object that 'nothing could be further from the methods of science'.[1] A newspaper or political party is not trying to make the sort of statement which is helpful in scientific explanation: it is trying to use relevant slogans in order to persuade: and those who suppose that it is doing anything else have not begun to understand it.

The fact is that Lady Wootton is persuading to what may, without too much exaggeration, be called a religion. The religion may be a barren and uncharitable one but it is a religion nevertheless. In her experience, she tells us in a moment of self-revelation, 'many students who have been brought up in a Christian, or other specifically religious state, and turn to the study of the social sciences, reach a point at which they are troubled by the difficulty of reconciling their religion and their scientific studies'.[2] If Lady Wootton is teaching them, however, why should one be surprised? If, whilst offering as academic explanation a body of anti-Christian dogma, Lady Wootton wants sufficient transparency to recognize the dogmatic character of her explanation; and if, as seems only too likely to be the case, she supposes it to be a function of 'science' to push back the area of religion, then the religious student will certainly be in confusion. Only if the limits of science are clearly grasped, only if its function is confined to explanation of the subject-matter under consideration and if claims are avoided which imply that political, moral or ethical science has authority to subvert religious commitment will this sort of confusion be avoided.

The opinions we have described are maintained by scholars who are responsible for the dominant manner

[1] *Testament*, p. 63.　　　[2] *Testament*, p. 117.

in the literature of the social and political sciences and who exert great influence in its teaching. The pretension to propose practical policies based on rational consideration, impartial judgement and freedom from prejudice, and the tendency to suppose that they are buttressed by academic authority, is connected with failure to see that no policy can in that sense be agreed to be rational, impartial or unprejudiced, and that all the causes to which scholars commit themselves can as much, and as little, be known to be the outcome of rational consideration as any maintained by anyone else. The author maintains opinions about the duties of government in relation to foreign policy, the citizen and public order suitable (if he cares to hold them) to anyone in his frame of mind, and attaches importance to the probability that the party to which he belongs will maintain these positions and enunciate these slogans for a considerable time in the future. He does not, however, pretend that disaster will follow if it does not or that these opinions flow in some readily discernible way from the nature of the universe, the dictate of the rational will, the judgement of common sense or any other of the phrases with which men dignify their approval of the courses they propose to take. They are, on the contrary, part of the furniture of his mind which will be suitable and sensible according to the way in which they are used and which he sees as little cause to change as his profession, his style of dressing or the books he reads. The use he makes of these slogans and the manner in which he commits himself to them is relevant in assessing his success in acting rightly or wrongly, rationally or irrationally. But though these things are important, he sees no reason in explanation to impute to them an intellectual necessity and moral priority he cannot possibly know them to have. Messrs Benn and Peters, on the other hand, in their *Social Principles and the Democratic State* produce ostensibly explanatory reasons for accepting liberal-democratic slogans about the connection between justice and impartiality, about the significance of universal suffrage, about the United Nations and about taxation according to need and desert without either recognizing their arbitrary character or asking on what grounds anybody should bother to accept them. When they claim[1] that 'Justice consists in treating equals equally, and in adopting as criteria by which men are to be considered equal or unequal, only such qualities or circumstances as can be reasonably justified', two questions must be asked. In the first place what is the content of 'reasonably'? And once one comes to the point of giving it content, is there likely to be agreement about it? 'Reasonable', 'rational' and 'impartial' are capable of innumerable varieties of content. In what circumstances is one to say that 'the criteria by which men are ... considered equal' are relevant or reasonable? The authors do not believe that pigmentation-criteria are: but is there anything in their explanation which makes this self-evident? If there is 'no formula for determining what differences are relevant', how is it that 'we can formulate principles of procedure, namely that particular distinctions must be sanctioned by rules and ... ultimately justified in terms of the generally beneficent consequences of adopting and maintaining them'.[2] One may agree that whilst a '[South African] judge may act justly in denying a man the vote because he has a black skin, if that is the law ... we can still question whether the criterion established by the law is itself defensible'.[3] This, however, should not stop us wondering why a legislator's

---

[1] S. I. Benn and R. S. Peters, *Social Principles and the Democratic State*, p. 135.
[2] Benn and Peters, p. 114.　　　　[3] Benn and Peters, p. 111.

preference for one sort of criterion—designed to support laws which, for example, give the vote to white men alone —have to be justified 'in terms of more general rules and ultimately of a balance of advantage to all concerned'.[1] 'The balance of advantage to all concerned' is a useful slogan with which to recommend laws that have already been enacted or proposals for bills that are about to be made public: but there is no reason why it should be thought a necessary one. It is open to every variety of interpretation: and it is not clear what authority the political scientist has in choosing it. If an apologist says bluntly that the restricted franchise is not intended to benefit the black population, what is the political scientist to answer? Is the rule that legislation should benefit the white population a 'general rule' in our authors' sense or is it not? If another apologist (of a subtler kind), whilst in private believing that a restricted franchise would not benefit the black population, argued nevertheless in public that it would, what would the position be then? And if, in attempting to humour the political scientist who believes that the relevant criterion must both be a general rule and issue 'ultimately . . . in a balance of advantage to all concerned', an apologist tried to meet both his requirements, would our political scientist accept the argument that, since God's Will is that White Civilization should survive in South Africa, and since also it is God's Will that God's Will should be obeyed: since, furthermore, obedience to God's Will must result 'ultimately' in 'a balance of advantage to all concerned' and since an extended franchise would imperil White Civilization, that therefore the form of disobedience to God's Will involved in giving the vote to Black men cannot be acceptable.

This, it will be said, is a persuasive syllogism, not an

[1] Benn and Peters, p. 112.

explanatory statement; an assertion, not a giving of reasons; and such a comment would be just. But it is no more a persuasive statement than the assertion that the criterion by which a law can be justified must be in terms 'ultimately . . . of a balance of advantage to all concerned'. Can the advantage of all not conflict with the advantage of each? And if it can, is this particular criterion capable of determining anything? Is it not as nebulous a concept as God's Will or the natural law? And can it be given such self-evidently specific content as to meet the accusation that it is used by our authors as a receptacle for every sort of arbitrary persuasion?

In fact, because they do not separate their practical political purpose from the explanatory one, one is compelled to conclude that these two authors make the error, in spite of specific avowals that they do not, of assuming that explanatory 'principles' can be used to make definitive evaluation of the rightness of the actions which governments take. It is not just the claim that 'morality arises when custom or law is subjected to critical examination' that is in question but the assumption that 'issues must be decided in the light of arguments and not because of the authority or personality or religion or social class of the person who propounds them'—as though the giving of reasons and provision of arguments, however competently conducted, were the only measure of the morality of actions not yet taken in the light of consequences not generally predictable, or as though, even if it were, this would free philosophers from the primacy of the obligation to turn back upon their 'principles' in order to ask what status these principles have.

Neither in practice nor in explanation can arbitrariness be escaped: no man can be totally transparent to himself. Nevertheless, in philosophy, transparency is the only object worth pursuing, and the more a writer sees his assumptions for what they are, the better for the progress of the activity. The worse, also, for its progress when writers fail in this sort of sensitivity. Mr Peters, for example, tells us[1] that whereas 'every religion rests on some sort of authoritative criterion, like the Bible, an *ex cathedra* utterance of a pope, or the revelation vouchsafed to an individual believer . . . moral beliefs . . . like scientific ones, must be rationally justified'. One is, however, tempted to suggest that the fundamental assumptions of 'morality' (which turns out in the next paragraph to be 'enlightened morality') rest on authoritative assumptions also. 'The spread of enlightenment' may, as Mr Peters suggests, have 'tended to disrupt and transform [authority] by insisting on reasons for policy rather than authoritative edicts, and by claiming that authority is only to be tolerated if it has some rational justification': but the authority which asks for 'reasons' and claims to be the guardian of 'rational justification' is no freer than any other of the tendency to make arbitrary assumptions. From these assumptions a structure of argument and justification does, it is true, develop: but so it does where the assumptions are the 'truths of christianity'. To anyone who does not accept the assumptions in the first place, the one set as much as the other will seem arbitrary persuasions to which commitment will come as much from upbringing, situation and habit as from anything Mr Peters would recognize as 'rational justification'. Nor does 'traditional authority' differ in this respect from 'science' and 'morality'. To think so is to ignore the extent to which 'traditional' governments produced reasons to justify themselves and to disregard the fact that enlightened political authorities are subject

[1] R. S. Peters, *Authority, Responsibility and Education* (1959), pp. 22–3.

to the difficulties which all established institutions face in maintaining themselves in existence. The assumptions of enlightenment, to which many contemporary governments are committed, need as much to be buttressed in practice by force, fraud, consent and committed belief as did any of the assumptions of their predecessors. When 'traditional' assumptions are overthrown, they are replaced, not by 'rationality', but by other assumptions: and it is only because Mr Peters is himself committed to these assumptions that he fails to see that 'science, morality, and enlightenment', so far from providing 'rational' norms, are in fact the persuasive slogans he happens to use in order to conceal the uncritical belief that *his* body of assumptions is not arbitrary at all. It is not *essential* to morality that 'we should consider proposals ... with *impartiality*'. A person is not *necessarily* 'immoral' who says that what 'is right for himself need not be right for somebody else'. It is not *everywhere* thought 'morally suspect' to believe that 'one ought always to further the interests of one's country, church or party',[1] though it is certainly ridiculous to offer a preference for the 'slogans of humanity' as though these slogans have explanatory content.

In one of these passages 'morality' is connected with 'relevance': but it is difficult to see what, in this connection, 'relevant' means. The answer, no doubt, is that a decision, in order to be right, must be relevant to the matters under consideration. In a formal sense, this is true (just as intentions which cannot possibly be performed cannot be right intentions to have). The difficulty is, however, that just as there is disagreement about what it *is* possible to do, so there is disagreement about what is relevant to a particular situation. Some

[1] Peters, p. 114.

people would argue that race or colour are relevant to the question—where ought a man to be allowed to walk in public?—but others would not. 'Science' provides no resolution of this difficulty: and failure to resolve the difficulty leaves us with nothing more than a tautologous truth without determinate content—the truth that a law cannot be right if it takes no account of the relevant circumstances. The dilemma from which the exponents of a scientific or rational morality think they have escaped is, indeed, inescapable. Either the reasons provided by scientific morality to support, or prohibit, a line of action are without content or they have any content men may happen to insert: and what looks like an escape from the arbitrary world of religious commitment provides nothing more than a persuasion to exchange one set of commitments for another. In practice it is no doubt a strength that Mr Peters's writing at this crucial point is dense and untransparent: but this does not alter the fact that density and untransparency reduce the value of his explanatory offerings.

We have so far extracted from the writings of prominent, contemporary political scientists passages which display, not the whole range of output of each, but examples of temptations to which even the most sensible succumb. It may, finally, be desirable to examine the account of the relationship between political practice and political science given by two scholars who, though differing in the language with which they support their practical commitments, yet share a common position. So far as they suppose that political science and political sociology should not only have explanatory functions, but should also deliberately concern themselves with possibilities of usefulness in political practice, these writers argue in a similar direction. Professor Popper and the late Professor Mannheim agree in little: the 'sociology of Knowledge' is a target of Professor Popper's criticism; but in their failure to grasp the limits which an academic setting imposes on all academic writing, the writings of both have the same misleading implications.

In asking why there is no Science of Politics Professor Mannheim first observes that there is a body of practical knowledge which, though useful for politicians in practice, does not merit the name of science.[1] With this we may agree. He then removes from the sphere of 'conduct' and 'politics' actions taken by officials in areas of social activity where regular rules operate and in which therefore 'life itself has already been rationalised and ordered'. This, though cautiously expressed, seems a little less reasonable, since it excludes from 'political activity' activity that is not new, problematical and purposive and under-estimates the significance of the fact that 'rules' which appear to be 'ordered and rationalised' not only change their character as time passes, but have consequences which alter profoundly as changes occur in the society in which they operate. Nevertheless, one may for the moment follow this diagnosis to the point at which, 'having determined where the realm of the truly political begins . . . we can indicate the difficulties existing in the relationship between theory and practice'.[2] And not only may it be accepted that the chief obstacle in the way of scientific knowledge of politics 'arises from the fact[3] . . . that we are . . . dealing . . . with tendencies and strivings in a state of flux' and from the fact that 'the observer himself does not stand outside the realm of the irrational, but is a participant in the conflict of forces': it may even be agreed that the first five examples in which ideological

---

[1] K. Mannheim, *Ideology and Utopia* (ed. 1960), p. 99.
[2] Mannheim, p. 103. [3] Mannheim, p. 103.

involvement is said to have deflected the political scientist from 'scientific' statement[1] did in fact have this effect.

Now an individual political scientist may, as Mannheim insisted, be operating in a social situation the limits of which his thought to some degree reflects. His thought is, however, not *completely* determined: the most important qualities that distinguish Marx from Dühring or Lenin from Trotsky are to be found, not in the condition of the society in which they lived, but, in the character of their several intellectual histories. Nor is it reasonable to suggest that 'if it be once granted that political thought is always bound up with a position in the social order, it is only consistent to suppose that the tendency towards a total synthesis must be embodied in the will of some social group'.[2] On the contrary, if by 'will' is meant the practical, social and political writings of some group, this will almost certainly limit the usefulness of the synthesis in explanation. Mannheim uses 'valid synthesis' to mean 'a political position which will constitute a progressive development in the sense that it will retain and utilize much of the accumulated cultural acquisitions and social energies of the previous epoch' and which will 'at the same time . . . permeate the broadest ranges of social life . . . and take . . . natural root in society in order to bring its transforming power into play': but the only effect of this will be to encourage practical preoccupation with the consequences of action to override the concern for explanation. The fact is that 'synthesis' in Mannheim's sense is part of a practical ideology, an occasion for the exercise of political power by the 'unanchored, *relatively* classless stratum'[3]—'the socially unattached intelligentsia' who, *because* they are socially unattached,

[1] Mannheim, pp. 105–36.   [2] Mannheim, p. 136.   [3] Mannheim, p. 137.

are assumed to be free from the disabling bias which class interest and social situation have inserted into the syntheses made by the theorists of 'bureaucratic conservatism, conservative historicism, liberal-democratic bourgeois thought, the socialist-communist conception and fascism'.[1]

Mannheim supposed that there were two positions open to the intellectual. The first—of attaching himself to a particular class—though recognized to be legitimate and said to have the effect of 'lift[ing] the conflict of interests to a spiritual plane' (whilst also involving 'empty glorification of naked interests by means of the tissues of lies spun by apologists'),[2] was not, in his view, in spite of 'a tendency . . . towards a dynamic synthesis', itself the accomplishment of this 'synthesis'. It was, as Mannheim conceived it, only through the second— through 'intellectuals . . . becoming aware of their own social position and the mission implicit in it' that synthesis could be achieved. This mission he conceived to be 'the discovery of the position from which a total perspective would be possible'—a total perspective which intellectuals can achieve more readily than others because 'a group whose class position is more or less definitely fixed [as the intellectuals' is not], already has its political viewpoint decided for it'.[3] Only, he says, in this way is it possible to connect political decisions with a 'total orientation'. And not only is this a function intellectuals may *like* to perform, but 'today more than ever it is expected of such a dynamic middle group that it will strive to create a forum outside the party schools *in which the perspective of and interest in the whole* [my italic] is safeguarded'.[4]

It might at first sight seem that the 'political science'

---

[1] Mannheim, p. 104.   [2] Mannheim, p. 142.   [3] Mannheim, p. 143.
[4] Mannheim, p. 144.

to which Mannheim was drawing attention was in its pursuit of comprehensiveness of the same sort as the explanatory science to which the present book is dedicated. This, however, is not the case. It is true that Mannheim's political science is uncommitted to any political party, and one may pardon the belief, expressed in Germany in the early nineteen-thirties, that as 'more and more party schools' (of political science) arise, addressing themselves 'exclusively to those whose political decisions have been made in advance by parties', it will be 'all the more desirable that an actual forum be established, whether it be in the universities or in specialised higher institutions of learning, which shall serve the pursuit of this advanced form of political science'.[1] Even if it is not 'the object of such a school to avoid arriving at political decisions', one may agree that 'there is a profound difference between a teacher who, after careful deliberation, addresses his students, whose minds are not yet made up, from a point of view which has been attained by careful thinking leading to a comprehension of the total situation and a teacher who is exclusively concerned with inculcating a party outlook already firmly established'.[2] One may even applaud the candour which admits that 'those who demand of politics as a science that it teaches norms and ends' are in fact demanding 'the denial of the reality of politics'. All these things may be applauded: but at the nodal point it is impossible to follow —the point at which it is supposed that the explanation given in 'non-party schools' is likely to deserve the name of 'total', or that anything in practice would necessarily follow from it if it did.

Implicit in *Ideology and Utopia* and surrounded there with cautious realization of the objections, but explicit in all of Mannheim's later work, is the belief that the

[1] Mannheim, p. 144.　　　[2] Mannheim, pp. 144–5.

function of explanatory writing, the purpose of the 'Sociology of Knowledge', is not just to show in what way each world-view is a product of class or environmental bias, and not merely to suggest that differences between one set of preferences and another can be explained 'sociologically', but, by replacing these partial explanations with total comprehensive ones, to persuade readers to what Mannheim conceived to be total, practical, unavoidable, political commitments. Mannheim justifies this by suggesting that some things *can* be explained only by those who have an itch for action: and this, though not always, may often be so. Mannheim's political preferences may have helped him to greater awareness of the danger of class and situational bias, but they led him to exaggerate the importance of the danger also. He appeared, indeed, almost to suppose that once the effect of class and social situation on explanation had been exposed, the major limitation had been overcome. There is, however, no reason to think that these are the only obstacles in the way of explanatory adequacy. Explanation is hampered by every other sort of practical commitment as well: though it is also, in one sense, positively fertilized by every sort of 'bias'—so long as the bias is directed to explaining the subject-matter, and not to making an impact on it.

Mannheim asserts, reluctantly perhaps, that 'planning' is 'inevitable' in 'modern society'. 'Inevitable' is a word which ought always to be suspected: but one may for the occasion accept it. Even if one does, however, is one likely to discern any academic purpose in the attempt 'through an analytical approach, by breaking the mystical concept of the uniqueness of an age into a sum of smaller factors and situations . . . to solve the riddle of what the nature of social configurations must be in a planned society so as to ensure the emergence and favourable development of differentiated personality'?[1] Is this not merely a turgid version of stock platform clichés about reconciling freedom with order? Do they amount to anything more than the pious expression of hopes, the generous expression of opinions? Is it not absurd to talk of 'analytical and empirical observations' in an essay which has very few specific examples? And is not the question asked, and answered, in terms of such indeterminate generality that nothing of consequence can follow?

It might be objected that these are passing examples —no more significant than the sales-talk given to the *Institute of Sociology and World University Service* in 1936 to the effect that in 'the moral and social transformation of mankind' to which the next centuries 'should be dedicated . . . very much depends upon whether we can —before it is too late—succeed in building a science of society'.[2] Unfortunately these are characteristic extracts: and anyone who reads *Freedom, Planning and Democratic Order* will find the whole work dedicated to practical pursuit of the most absurd of sociological illusions—a total, impartial political science which, whilst leaving to others the act of decision, will though increased knowledge of the 'interrelations of social position, motives and points of view' 'enable us . . . not only to calculate more precisely collective interests and their corresponding modes of thought' but also to advance from the stage reached by Max Weber—'the stage in ethics and politics in which blind fate seems to be at least partially in the course of disappearance in the social process and the knowledge of everything knowable becomes the obligation of the acting person'.[3]

[1] *Essays in Sociology and Social Psychology* (1953), p. 280.
[2] *Essays in Sociology and Social Psychology*, p. 195.
[3] *Ideology and Utopia*, pp. 169, 171.

The 'Sociology of Knowledge' forms no part of Professor Popper's methodological equipment: but that does not prevent him being as much concerned as Mannheim with the practical responsibilities of political science. In *The Poverty of Historicism*, he distinguishes between two possible views of the function of the social sciences. There is the view that 'social science is nothing but history'. Of this he says, rightly, that where this means 'the kind of history with which historicists wish to identify sociology'—the kind which 'looks not only backwards to the past but also forwards to the future' in order to 'formulate hypotheses about general trends underlying social development, in order that men may adjust themselves to impending changes by deducing prophecies from these laws'—it is compatible with the view that 'sociological experiments are useless and impossible'.[1] This is the 'utopian' or 'holistic' approach: it is attacked throughout *The Poverty of Historicism* and *The Open Society and Its Enemies*: the only point to make about it for the moment is that it is a philosophical doctrine rather than a way of writing history. The second view of the function of the social sciences is called 'the piecemeal view'—the view that 'in opposition to the historicist methodology, we could conceive of a methodology which aims at a *technological social science*', leading to 'the study of the general laws of social life with the aim of finding all those facts which would be indispensable as a basis for the work of everyone seeking to reform social institutions'.[2]

In arguing this position Professor Popper avoids the obvious objections. Far from accusing 'historicists' of suggesting that '*nothing* can be brought about' by deliberate social purpose, he seems (if he does not quite accept) to have some sympathy with the view that 'neither your dreams nor what your reason constructs will be ever

[1] K. R. Popper, *The Poverty of Historicism*, pp. 44–6.   [2] Popper, p. 46.

brought about according to plan'.[1] Nevertheless, he shows an imperfect grasp of the limits of an academic subject. In his anxiety to dispose of the historicist persuasion to conform to the inevitable march of history, he fails to be articulately sensitive about the fact that his own counter-persuasion—to piecemeal social engineering —is a persuasion to action also. Merely because the 'historicist' uses one slogan—the inevitable march of history—in order to justify his practical preferences, it should not be supposed that the logic of *his* statement is different from the logic of Professor Popper's. No greater certainty about the practical consequences will be achieved by adopting one view of the social sciences than by adopting the other. Professor Popper supposes that 'utopian holism' combined with 'historicism' produces totalitarian government, but there is no reason to think it does. Consequences are affected by every sort of cause besides intention: and the language of 'piecemeal engineering', no more than the language of 'utopian prediction', will relieve governments of the chances to which all government is liable.

The criticism Professor Popper is making of historicism is not that its exponents are too much concerned with the practical task of the social sciences but that, in achieving the practical results which it claims to achieve, 'historicism . . . [is] a poor method'.[2] At one point in *The Poverty of Historicism*, Professor Popper asserts that 'the defenders of the rights of "pure" or "fundamental" research deserve every support in their fight against the narrow view, unfortunately again fashionable, that scientific research is justified only if it proves to be a sound investment'.[3] This seems admirable. But as soon as one asks—what is the pure research in the social

---

[1] Popper, p. 49.   [2] Popper, p. 58.   [3] Popper, p. 55.

8   113

sciences to which he wants support to be given?—the answer once more is '"piecemeal tinkering" (as it is sometimes called) combined with critical analysis . . . through attempts to find out whether or not some particular economic or political action is likely to produce an expected or desired result . . . investigations into the effects of prison reform or universal health insurance, or of the stabilisation of prices by means of tribunals, or of the introduction of new import duties etc., upon say, the equalisation of incomes . . . and [such] urgent questions . . . as the possibility of controlling trade cycles . . . the question whether centralised "planning", in the sense of state management of production, is compatible with an effective democratic control of the administration, or the question of how to export democracy to the Middle East'.[1] Again it is recognized that one value of 'piecemeal tinkering' is that 'it is likely to prove fruitful in giving rise to significant problems of a purely theoretical kind', and again this is excellent. But once more it is clear also that an important object of this sort of enquiry is the formulation of policy. No one can deny that the findings of social scientists are used extensively by government: but social scientists themselves have no obligation to the problems of policy. Professor Popper, in an attempt to be fair to 'historicism', adduces the fact that many historicists have believed in the desirability of practical reform: but this is of no academic consequence. It does not matter, academically speaking, whether Professor Popper has an 'activist' or 'anti-interventionist' idea of what to do about the social order. Both attitudes are commitments to practice; neither is relevant to the academic concern or judgeable by its authority. What matters, indeed the only thing academically that does matter, is the attitude he takes to the only question of

[1] Popper, p. 59.

importance—what idea a scholar should have of the way in which society works.

Professor Popper seems sometimes to confine himself within explanatory limits, but the appearance is deceptive. The examples he gives[1] of the analogy between 'sociological laws and hypotheses' and 'the laws or hypotheses of the natural sciences' leave, as he rightly observes, 'much room for improvement' but we may agree that some of them, if formulated more accurately, would deserve consideration. It may, for example, be true that 'you cannot introduce agricultural tariffs and at the same time reduce the cost of living', that 'you cannot in an industrial society organise consumers' pressure groups as effectively as you can organise certain producers' pressure groups', or that 'you cannot have full employment without inflation'. Since these are offered as examples of the *sort* of statements which amount to sociological laws rather than as actual laws themselves, there is no need to investigate their content here. They do, however, one may agree, deserve investigation. But can one say of the set 'taken from the realm of power politics' that they deserve investigation at all? Would it amount to anything more than the highest political gossip to 'discuss', and suppose that by discussing one could 'substantiate',[2] such hypotheses as that 'You cannot introduce a political reform without strengthening the opposing forces, to a degree roughly in ratio to the scope of the reform', that 'you cannot make a revolution without causing a reaction', that 'you cannot make a successful revolution if the ruling class is not weakened by internal dissension or defeat in war' or that 'you cannot give a man power over other men without tempting him to misuse it—a temptation which roughly increases

[1] Popper, pp. 62-3.
[2] Popper, p. 63.

with the amount of power wielded and which very few are capable of resisting'?

Objection could be raised to the manner of formulation but the question that matters for our purpose is—what are such hypotheses for? Are they intended to be guides to action or aids to explanation? The answer is, quite clearly, in Professor Popper's mind, both. Why otherwise, does he add to one hypothesis—'You cannot introduce a political reform without causing some repercussions which are undesirable from the point of view of the ends aimed at'—the injunction 'and therefore look out for them'? Not only are they hypotheses of an explanatory sort which a piecemeal technology may attempt (in an explanatory manner) to 'substantiate', but a reason for substantiating them is to provide suggestions about the policies governments ought to follow. In criticizing the 'holist' who, instead of fighting against 'the greatest and most urgent evils of society ... [like] ... poverty and unemployment', seeks only 'some ultimate good', he argues that 'if [the piecemeal technologist or engineer] ... wishes to introduce scientific methods into the study of society and into politics, what is needed most is the adoption of a critical attitude, and the realisation that not only trial but also error is necessary'.[1] But there is here also a considerable confusion—the belief that enunciation of a different set of slogans about action ensures that a corresponding sort of action will ensue. Hitler used holistic language: Hitler may be said to have wanted the 'State' to control 'society': but Hitler nevertheless fought against the greatest and most urgent evils of society, 'poverty and unemployment', and by using Dr Schacht to deal with them provided an admirable example of 'piecemeal social engineering'.

One difference, as Professor Popper sees it, between

---

[1] Popper, pp. 87–8.

the 'holistic' and the 'piecemeal' approach is that 'while the piecemeal engineer can attack his problem with an open mind as to the scope of the reform, the holist cannot do this: for he has decided beforehand that a complete reconstruction is possible and necessary'. Of this, however, one may ask whether 'totalitarian' politicians do in practice act so very differently from those who are aiming at 'piecemeal social engineering'. Mr Khrushchev seems to learn by his mistakes. Stalin, who almost certainly believed total reconstruction to be necessary in the Soviet Union in 1924, almost certainly had an 'open mind' about its content. It is possible that the point at which his mind was closed was the point at which many other Russian statesmen, aiming in the same situation to maintain Russian independence, would have closed theirs also. And is there not a danger that Professor Popper, in anxiety to honour the 'memory of the countless men and women of all creeds or nations or races' whom he supposes to have fallen victim to the 'fascist and communist belief in the Inexorable Laws of Human Destiny',[1] has forgotten that the complications of action are so great that it is idle to impute to any particular doctrine responsibility for the consequences, and misleading to suppose that, in the dislocation caused by the breakdown of the East European polity after 1918, doctrines different from the ones that were adopted would necessarily have been more agreeable. It is not necessarily the case that 'the question whether we adopt some more or less radical form of irrationalism, or whether we adopt that minimum concession to irrationalism which I have termed "critical irrationalism" will deeply affect our whole attitude towards other men and towards the problems of social life'.[2] It may do, if we mistake the function of an explanatory tool: but there is no reason

[1] Popper, p. v.   [2] *The Open Society and Its Enemies* (1945), p. 219.

why it should. 'Rationalism', in its explanatory aspect, may have been used by those who wish to see mankind 'united'. 'The fact that [irrationalism] may easily be combined with . . . a romantic belief in the existence of an elect body in the division of men into leaders and led'[1] may, perhaps, justify Professor Popper's claim that 'a moral decision is involved in the choice between it and rationalism'—but only in the sense that all decisions of every sort are under judgement. There is no reason to suppose that 'irrationalistic' explanation of the character of human action will produce undesirable historical consequences: and if there were, that would say nothing about its utility, and nothing against using it, in explanation.

Actions indeed, which at one level seem 'irrational', may well in the ultimate perspective turn out to be rational. Professor Popper's assumption that intentions in order to be 'rational' have to be self-conscious humanitarian, egalitarian ones by-passes the question whether emotional, instinctive reactions in different directions may not be 'rational' also. At one moment[2] Professor Popper is cautious.[3] At another he is not.[4] But, whatever the tone, the assumption remains that a relevant criticism of a body of explanation is that it produces undesirable consequences in practice and that Professor Popper thinks it legitimate to remark of thinkers who have concluded that human action is controlled by self-conscious purpose less than men sometimes like to think, that 'this irrational emphasis upon emotion and

---

[1] *The Open Society and Its Enemies* (1945), p. 219.

[2] *The Open Society and Its Enemies* (1945), p. 221.

[3] 'I do not intend to say that the adoption of this humanitarian attitude of impartiality [between men] is a direct consequence of a decision in favour of rationalism.'

[4] 'But I do wish to stress the fact that the irrationalist attitude can hardly avoid becoming entangled with the attitude that is opposed to equalitarianism' because of 'its [rationalism's] emphasis upon the emotions and passions: [and because] we cannot feel the same emotions towards everybody.' *The Open Society and Its Enemies* (1945), p. 222.

passion leads ultimately to what I can only describe as crime'.[1] Is any *explanatory* purpose served by observations of this kind? Is any academic function performed by remarking that 'the adoption of an anti-egalitarian attitude in political life . . . is just what I should call criminal'? And do these pages not demonstrate that the claim made by Professor Popper that 'the only course open to [the social sciences] is to tackle the practical problems of our time with the help of the theoretical methods which are fundamentally the same in all the sciences' means not that these methods should be used within the academic subject-matter in order to explain the fact that men do in practice 'tackle the practical problems of our time', but that they are the methods appropriate to the social scientist in attempting to accumulate practical authority in order to tackle political problems themselves?

The confusions we have described so far produce a range of discussion which inculcates the belief that political activity is more predictably responsive to self-conscious purpose than it can be: with the result that when remedies for contemporary difficulties are proposed, they are supposed to be more essential than in fact they are. It ignores the fact that politics is an uncertain, broken-backed activity which is saved from triviality chiefly by the ambition of politicians, the continuity of habits and institutions and the permanent interests of persons and groups: and that almost all public discussion, from our ignorance of the future and the difficulty of anticipating the accidents of political decision, decides not what is to be done (though that is the conventional pretence maintained), but which party or group shall command sufficient support to make the decisions. Nor

[1] *The Open Society and Its Enemies* (1945), p. 223.

does this apply to politicians seeking office alone. The great organs of impartiality (the B.B.C. for example) are by their choice of information constantly asserting, equally with any politician, the right to affect policy: and if political parties may be rejected because of the slogans they use, may not these authorities be rejected for these reasons also? Anyone who wants political authority must expect to get it, not in proportion to his knowledge (for so many political decisions are taken in the dark) but so far as he can make his audience assent. There is no necessary reason why professors of philosophy, sociology or law (or the editor of *The Times*) should be thought of as authorities when they criticize the hanging, euthanasia, abortion or homosexuality laws: or the Vice-Chancellor of a university (who has never been to South Africa) when he talks about the policies of the South African Government. In all these matters scholars, as much as anyone else, are slaves to habit. Addiction to the pretension to tell men how to organize their lives or direct their society is pleasanter than understanding what political activity is like: but between the two activities there is little connection and professional standing in one provides no basis for authority in the other.

From all that has been said so far, what conclusions can be drawn? In the first place it is desirable to rid university faculties of the pretension to be schools of political practice, not because of the confusion this induces in the conduct of politics, but because of the damage it does to universities themselves. Although politicians can digest the errors of dons, universities are less happily placed. If dons mistake their function there, nothing will save the teaching faculties from falling into decay. A university faculty is a place where dons teach those things which they understand better than anyone else, and if faculties are set up on any other basis, damage will be done. Members of university faculties can normally know so little about the way contemporary politics works that little can be said for regarding contemporary government as a subject for academic study and nothing at all for thinking it will throw light on the nature of political activity in general. The only school of political practice is the conversation of those who govern, but their conversation is not carried on in public: and even if it were, it might only disclose what they think they are doing, which so far from invariably being what they do do, is as likely to be what Dicey, Bagehot or Sir Ivor Jennings have told them their predecessors were doing thirty years before. It follows from this that, whilst fictional reconstruction of well-attested public events may often throw light on the way in which events occur (though without possibility of verification), little advantage can come from the pseudo-scientific writings of those who pretend, without making names, to explain the workings of the institutions of government. A statesman (with a reflective turn of mind) may always make a contribution to political thought, though few in fact do. But in universities three sorts of study only are likely to be fruitful—history, through which the evidences left by men in the past are explained, not in a generalized, but in a specific way (by naming names): economic theory: and a metaphysical subject-matter which, in ways that will become apparent in a moment, embraces and subdues such constituent subjects (like social psychology, general sociology and jurisprudence) as have of late in English universities become independent of it.

The difficulties in the way of providing consistent illumination are great—greater than is commonly supposed. The patches that any generation lights up are likely to be few. The wastage (in unrewarding writing) is likely to be great: and success (which is never likely to come easily) will never come at all to those who slide smoothly across the surface of events or mistake the dilemmas of a moralizing intelligentsia for serious explanation of the world as it is. Difficult, however, or not, such illumination is much more likely when those who pretend to give it descend from the high places on which political ideals are postulated, political doctrines promulgated and political advice given in order to see what happens to intentions, ideals, doctrines and advice once they have taken their chance in a vast and unpredictable world. If the descent is not made, writing is likely to be flat, stale and uncritical. Once it is made, the uncritical arrogance of improving liberalism is likely to be curbed, and the advice that it gives and the purposes it proposes seem to be no more than pious hopes, expressions of the merest opinion which may or may not turn out to be suitable as chance and the energy of its advocates determine. In England today, political writing—of the practical and of the reflective kind—is under the domination of an imprecise literary liberalism which, because it makes no attempt to explore the deficiences of its experience, does not realize its limitations. Exploration of this kind, however, is important—more important, than anything else. For it might, on the one hand, induce a certain self-criticism in the minds of those who treat a society which all men have made as though it had been laid out for disposition by *them*. And it might on the other make clearer than it usually is the distinction between the ambition to 'master' the world by understanding it (which is the central academic undertaking) and the practical pretension to master the world by improving it, whose source is a misunderstanding about the nature of political science and which has in fact done, is indeed still doing, great damage to political thought whatever its effect on political practice.

II

IN ENGLISH history the range of writing designed to fulfil the practical function has always been extensive. It has its use in displaying to men, who wish to have opinions about political action, the implications of the positions to which they are committed, and is helpful in developing a political casuistry by which men are enabled to see what political choices are implied by the particular prejudices they happen to maintain. There is, however, no reason why the authority of sensitive consciences or articulate pens should supersede the authority of anyone else: and failure to be interested in the practical limitations of this sort of authority reinforces the conclusion that the views propounded and the attitudes expressed are defective as explanation also. But, we must ask, if they have no absolute validity, have these statements *any* validity? And we must answer: as political philosophy they have none whatever: as historical explanation none at all: and as slogans they must be judged to have more or less according to the attention which men who are engaged in practice are willing to give them. Injunctions to establish rules of equality or impartiality are statements in political practice and designed to have political consequences. Justifications (in terms of principle) of particular arrangements for distributing property have temporary utility to those who want to maintain a particular set of political arrangements, but provide no substitute for historical or philosophical explanation of their nature. Accounts of the workings of contemporary institutions and comparisons between systems of government give only the baldest outline of how institutions work or governments operate and are wanting, almost always in Britain, in the central information on which explanation can be built. Undertakings of this sort dissolve under scrutiny, on the one hand, into injunctions to action (which it is not the professional business of university teachers to provide) and on the other, into the barest provision of guide-book information, useful to journalists as they write, or to politicians as they speak in public. But of the uncertainty involved in political action, there is no hint whatever. Of the gap which the nature of the world imposes on the accomplishment of any political purpose, nothing at all. And of the great, many and varied difficulties which attend the effort to see the world as it is, with all its difficulties and limitations and without regard to the desire to alter it, they show such disregard as to alienate serious attention. To the question, therefore, to what object should serious attention be directed, it is necessary now to turn.

The first task, the central problem of political reflection, is to distinguish statements relevant to practice from statements relevant to philosophy. This is necessary not because confusion does damage to practice but because of the damage it does to philosophy. Robespierre's or Lenin's exaggerated expectations about the scope of political action may have contributed to violent breakdown in the French or Russian Revolutions. But none of the misconceptions of statesmen about the world they inhabit damage practice as much as philosophers' misconceptions distort philosophy. Philosophy is thought without arrest or limitation, explanation with as few assumptions as possible: or, if loaded with assumptions, then as coherent as words and thought permit. Its status lies in its character as thought, in the belief that what is thought to be the case has validity (in creating an intellectual world) and in the certainty that a world of this sort has conventions and customs, pitfalls and drawbacks of its own by their success in circumventing which philosophers and other creators of intellectual worlds can alone properly be judged. The problems that emerge and the explanations which are given arise from the difficulty Mind has in accepting the world it lives in: from the limitations it experiences on satisfaction of its wishes; and from the fact that the world it sees is different from the world it would like to see around it. Instead of a world of peace and concord, instead of a world at one with itself, instead of a world of response to every desire that is expressed, it sees a world of strife and conflict where desires are thwarted and wishes unfulfilled, and where its own particular satisfactions can be provided not by attempting to remove but only by attempting to account for the difficulties. It is best conducted without concern for the consequences in practice and it can in this respect, in the hands of those who misunderstand its relevance, be subversive—not just of the political institutions it is often improperly employed to judge but of the pragmatic certainties that action needs. Political philosophy extends its probing destructiveness everywhere and is likely to be offensive to those in one direction who pretend to know that the policies they happen to prefer embody with greater exactitude than anything else the Will of God, the law of nature or absolute right, and is likely in another to disappoint those who pretend to know that existing institutions are in conflict with them. Its tendency is never to support one arrangement or principle rather than another, but to be a constant reminder that philosophy must present any set of political arrangements and all political principles as conjoined simples, complexes of arbitrary attitudes and opinions embedded in established institutions and having specific histories of their own, but with only the most uncertain claim to embody truth, right, goodness or rationality more effectively than everything else in human history. Those who practise this style of philosophy will find no ground to attach its name to one political party or group in preference to another. Enunciation of reasons for supporting one party or another, or advocating one set of policies rather than another, is a part of political practice involving a manipulation of thoughts, a juggling of slogans within a world of prejudice and action whose exponents are accustomed to this sort of activity. But writing of this sort geared to persuade to particular courses of political action has none of the character of philosophy, none of its unconcern for the consequences and is wholly without that obsession with consistency and coherence which the activity of explanation alone can give to those who pursue it. This, no doubt, is an arbitrary conception of political philosophy (though not as arbitrary as some): but it is not for that reason to be rejected. It, no more than any other human activity, can claim freedom from the imperfection of the human intelligence or the urge to pick up manners of thinking, by chance, instinct or situation as much as anything else, in order to see whether they can be used in practice to explain its limitations.

Political philosophy, then, is the outcome of Mind reflecting upon itself and its first task is to explore its limits, to ask what it knows and be sure that it neither assumes nor asserts as truth what it can neither know nor recognize as more than tentative explanation of what it may hope to explain more clearly in the future. Metaphysical explanation on this basis has temporary validity, useful to the generation which gives it so far as it is coherent and has meaning. It does not solve problems once and for all: and failure to solve problems once and for all is not a disabling limitation. Each generation—and within each generation each tradition of thinking—finds difficulties that need discussion, creases that need ironing in the philosophy it inherits from the past: and if all the difficulties and all the creases dissolve into the perennial philosophical problems, that does not make it any less necessary that they should be dealt with in an idiom appropriate to the time and place in which they emerge. Political philosophy, in other words, is explanation written by those who write books for their own benefit and the benefit of those who read them. But not everybody who engages in political practice feels the need: and even when they do, they not infrequently convert to practical use the arguments advanced in them. So uncertain is the field of practical influence open to the political philosopher, indeed, that it may be wisest (if the integrity of the subject-matter is to be preserved) for philosophers to avoid the attempt to control it altogether.

Nor is to be assumed that work emerging from these conventions (of writing, argument, teaching and discussion) is more desirable than any other sort of human activity. The *use* of political philosophy is seldom obvious. That it is useful in practice to see the world for what it is, is too optimistic an assumption; too much authority need not be claimed for an activity which justifies itself in practice chiefly by providing scope for the disciplined development of individual thinkers and the possibility of a disciplined education. This is the social utility of political, and of all other sorts of, philosophy: that it helps in that process of disciplining the intellectual energies on which some part of society's health depends. European civilization has rested heavily on clarity of thought and clarity of expression and the conscientious reluctance to assert that to be so which clearly is not.

Higher education in England for many generations past has been designed to enable pupils to say neither more nor less than they understand about questions of intrinsic difficulty: and if any consequential justification is sought for the energy scholars have devoted to cultivating subject-matters of this sort, this must be it. Explanation has conventions and requirements of its own which enable scholars to do what they can to ensure that the subject they teach is as honest as they can make it: and although one need not expect from this sort of achievement more than it can bring, it has, at any rate, consequences of a sort. And it may be that a society which fails to cultivate the academic competence may tend to misunderstand the world around it: its libraries and laboratories may empty; it may in time lose that control over nature which sustained, disciplined and controlled intelligence (fertilized by reflective insight) alone permits.

Extensive reflection, however, though stimulating many of the successes, and much of the damage, achieved by Western Europe, is not an essential feature of well-adjusted human societies. Many societies have existed in which self-conscious moral and intellectual culture has been thin, and philosophers would be wrong who, gifted with reflective intelligence (and suffering also the disabilities that go with it), pretend that those who are without it cannot lead lives as meticulously ordered, as well-regulated or as morally appropriate as any lived by the most cultivated citizen of the most cultivated State in Europe. Articulate doctrine is no *necessary* mark of effective (or good) government, though it has played *a* part in the government of the country in the last hundred years. Those who come to government after a lifetime of fighting or farming are as likely to govern sensibly as those who come to it after a life of philosophy (though all three may well defer to those who spend their lives preparing to govern). There is here the danger of romantic cant—the temptation to suppose that the inarticulate are for that reason better citizens than any other: but it is not being suggested that farmers, competence being equal, are necessarily better for this purpose than philosophers. Nevertheless, though it matters that political philosophy, if it is to be conducted at all, should be conducted sensibly, it is doubtful whether the undertaking is as essential to good government as the intrinsic difficulty of doing it might suggest.

The exercise of the reflective intelligence, then, is neither morally superior to, nor pragmatically more useful than, any of the other activities in which men are prone to pass their time. It is something men engage in if they choose to with no more importance than most activities and much less importance than some. In particular, it need not be suggested that philosophers have authority to undermine the certainty with which the majority of men engage in politics, believe religions, pursue interests, do good, procreate and live as men have usually done in civilized societies. If philosophers in the past have influenced these activities, the influence has been incidental: and nothing in the philosopher's task entitles him to expect to exert an influence in practice in the future. Preparation, furthermore, suitable for one sort of activity is not necessarily suitable for another: and if political philosophy is to be conducted and political activity seen in relation to other sorts of activity, its central functions must be differentiated from activities which bear a deceptive resemblance to it. The differentiation with which we have been concerned—between its legitimate character as explanation and a spurious character attributed to it in political discussion of providing guidance for action—does not mean that there are no substantive political principles relevant to political action, but merely that it is not the function of the political philosopher to provide them. His function, on the contrary, is to bring to the field of human activity with which he is dealing and of which they are a part, the desire to see it and them in relation to all other human activities and to conduct himself, not with the pragmatic persuasiveness of moral leadership, but with a power of disciplined contemplation suitable to philosophy. Political philosophy, in this sense, is a branch of moral philosophy: but moral philosophy is not concerned with the enunciation of moral rules or the designation of moral truths: and any attempt to make it will do great damage.

Now this, neither a new nor eccentric position, will in some quarters seem an invitation to immorality and scepticism. One of the commonest errors in political philosophy is to suppose that unless a general rule, maxim or principle is actually formulated to justify a course of action, the action itself must necessarily be wanting in moral value. Since also, it has been supposed that provision of moral maxims is a task suitable to philosophy, it may be thought that the position maintained here might undermine morality by denying the possibility of moral judgement. While, however, it is not the function of the political philosopher to determine what should be done in practice, there most certainly are moral standards to which action should conform. Right and wrong, good and evil, virtue and vice in political as in individual moral contexts are words which have real and commanding content. Obviously and most certainly there are such standards and it is important that citizens should give effect to them. But the rightness of actions resides in the consequences as well as the intentions: the consequences of actions do not yield more readily to reflective thought than to any other: and so little does action yield itself to the particular competence of the political philosopher that those who engage in political action will usually find better advice (and he better employment) elsewhere. A man's moral principles will be influenced by the sort of picture of the world he has: but this influence is seldom mediated directly. It operates obscurely and deviously, not according to a simple correlation between seeing what things are like and acting on that knowledge, whilst the picture itself comes from many sources besides the political philosophy, or even the whole formal education, a man has been given. Moral action is not necessarily tied to straining after moral perfection in every instance: it comes as often as not from a process of relaxed education in which thought, organizing itself solely with a view to understanding, is likely to be most helpful, and where the philosopher will find that the giving of practical advice will have returns almost inversely proportional to the distraction it involves. It is, indeed, at moments when concern for the consequences of action is dead that formulation of whatever men can understand of the nature of the world is most likely to be effective.

Nor are the misconceptions which conceal these truths local, temporary or transient. They lie at the root of almost all contemporary political science. Even when its advocates are most modest, they betray the belief that political freedom consists, not in opening out an infinitude of possibilities about which prediction is impossible in advance, but in pursuing a premeditated course unequivocally knowable to the literate, educated or enlightened leaders of society and to those who have promulgated a particular political doctrine: and which is a moral imperative binding on all men independently of their status, character, situation and wishes because it follows necessarily from a coherent political philosophy.

In the great ideologies the philosophical claims are so absurd that they can with little intellectual effort be disposed of. But the idolatry which attaches universal validity to transitory positions extends beyond the totalitarian ideologies into the citadels of improving liberalism itself. The régimes established in Germany after 1933 and in Russia after 1917 used their control of the organs of propaganda in order to impute to a set of arbitrary slogans a universal necessity and a status in morality they cannot possibly be known to have had. In South Africa the moral certainty with which the doctrines of apartheid are enunciated by their clerical proponents involves the imputation of necessity to principles which their status as pragmatic justifications of practical policies does not support. These things are well understood. But is the moral and intellectual opposition to apartheid so very much different? Are not the slogans of racial equality and social justice, as presented in this (and in most other) contexts, examples of political idolatry also? Is there not a tendency for the supporters of 'liberal values' to impute to their transitory preferences a capacity to embody the moral law as dogmatic as that maintained by the supporters of the Dutch Reformed Church? Does not the verbal battle of the last four years reveal merely one set of absolute principles in the hands of one set of well-intentioned idealists confronting another set of absolute principles in the hands of another set of idealists whose claims are as idolatrous as those made by the South African Government itself? Behind the slogans there lies, it is true, a reality of fear and passion, a conflict of interest and clash of power which demand exercise of the practical intelligence. No doubt also a desire to affect events enjoins tactical exaggeration of the rightness of the opposed positions. No doubt it is necessary to claim certainty if action is to be undertaken, and no doubt claims necessary for practical purposes get carried over into philosophical ones. But do these accidents justify philosophers in taking the consequent philosophy seriously? Marx, it is true, did: but Marx had a coherent, if mistaken, view of the connection between practice and philosophy in which the contrast was dissolved. If, however, we are not to argue that a special sort of action is the *necessary* outcome of any particular philosophy, do the philosophical justifications with which action tends to be surrounded have any validity at all? Do they justify the claim of any party to any particular conflict to speak with the certain authority of incontrovertible truth? No one writing today about the conflict between Luther and the Papacy, Catholic and Protestant, Napoleon and the British or Louis XIV and the continental allies, would pretend that Luther, the Protestants, the Pitts and William III represented a right that was necessary or unequivocal. Nor would any serious historian now presume to judge between the rectitude attaching to what Charles V would have thought the political principles which flowed necessarily from his religion, and the necessary political principles to which Luther, in the course of his erratic political life, found himself committed. But if historians would not presume to arrogate to themselves this sort of judgement, is there any reason why philosophers or political scientists should try to either? And should not the variations of opinion (and even the variations of opinion held with fanatical certainty) make those, whose function it is to explain, cautious of commitment to all political certainties?

We are, indeed, presented as we look out upon the world with the spectacle of men, creeds, attitudes and opinions in conflict with one another. And the conflict is not only chronic, it is also unavoidable. Anyone who is engaged in action (if only the action of writing a book, giving a lecture or making a speech) knows that if men are to act at all they have to believe that what they are doing at any particular moment has a right sufficient to them in their own situations—even if not to all men in all situations. In the moment of action, at the point of decision, it is idle to ask whether Britain deserves to be defended, whether Napoleon ought to be resisted, whether the Turk, though Muslim, does not represent a civilization equal to that of the Balkan Christians whose interests he threatens: or whether a book which has to be finished might not have been better if the author's assumptions had been different. In action men do things without reflection, in virtue of what they are so far as they are capable of doing them: and reflection in these conditions can be inhibiting and subversive. This does not stop action being right or wrong or prevent the operation of the judgement of God. Nor does it make it easier to know what is right and what wrong and how that judgement will fall. This is true not just of action in a self-consciously rational manner but of all sorts of action, whatever the language used to justify it. The most altruistic liberal has his own irreducible commitment like anyone else and the right meditated by the conscience, whatever the damage it does to settled habit, is a rock on which every sort of pressure can bear without effect. The most latitudinarian rationalist has assumptions he will not abandon and adherence to causes, creeds, shibboleths, opinions (and habits, customs and institutions), though they can on occasion in the wrong hands and in the wrong causes (and sometimes no doubt in the right ones) profoundly disrupt the world, provide also the bedrock of prejudice and commitment, closed mind and decided judgement, which alone enable institutions and society to survive the changes of fashion to which the intellectual history of mankind is subject. In England it is not necessary to be assured of Britain's capacity for maintaining 'liberal or democratic values' before resenting encroachments from the Soviet Union (for encroachments from 'liberal' states could be resented equally). Commitments and causes of this sort can properly be supported as intellectual prejudices (without reason or excuse). There is in fact little agreement amongst men about what is right; no greater authority can be attributed to one set of commitments because they flow from the conviction or intuition of one group of men than to another; and a prejudice will be a rational one, not according to the success its supporters have in deciding that it is so, but so far as they have struck lucky, done right or chosen rationally without knowing it. A 'rational prejudice' will seem an intolerable paradox only if it is supposed that rationality must be judged by deliberate premeditation and rational intention, or when it is denied that what seems to an unsympathetic observer to be an arbitrary prejudice may well turn out to have a rational place within the framework of God's Providence. In making themselves at home in the world, men gain great comfort from pretending that they are able infallibly to discern rationality: but this ought not to blind philosophers to the obligation to recognize that their principles do not possess this sort of authority.

If the object here were to engage in political action, to affect the way men act or bring predictable alteration in the way they live, nothing further need be said—except to urge men to join one party rather than another, to engage in one profession rather than another, or parade one set of prejudices rather than another in the hope that these choices would be successful in the world and meet the requirements of an ultimate reckoning

135

thereafter. That, however, is not the intention. The object, on the contrary, is to suggest that none of the positions thought necessary to the maintenance of political society can be known to be embodiments of an absolutely right judgement which flows from philosophy: and that as, on the one hand in the contemplation of the history of mankind, nothing can be deduced except what men have thought it best to do, so nothing, on the other, can be deduced from philosophical explanation except understanding of the arbitrary, relative character of the causes and slogans to which men commit themselves in time in face of the absolutely exact, but in a philosophical context absolutely unknowable, judgement of God. This does not make it any the less true that some actions are right and some wrong: but it makes nonsense of philosophers' claims to know which are which. To the question: is human sacrifice immoral? what has the philosopher to say? And the answer is: nothing whatever. This example is extreme, it may be suggested: if one comes nearer home, the philosopher will speak more clearly. But when, nearer home, one asks: is the minimum wage desirable? the philosopher's advice, though more pressing, has no greater authority in practice merely because the judgement is made by a philosopher and has in any case no relevance at all to *his* concern since it is a question he is not equipped, as a philosopher, to answer. To call loyalty to the United Nations a 'higher' loyalty than loyalty to a nation-state is a persuasive judgement in political practice. 'Higher' is often used with equal appropriateness of the loyalty shown by a citizen to the State in which he lives and 'subversive' (according to the direction of one's prejudices) for commitment to any other organization. It is not the political philosopher's business to decide which is the more 'rational': nor is it his task to judge those who imply that one loyalty must necessarily be 'higher' than the other. Men do in practice make this sort of claim, and to suggest that they should not is to engage in practice also. The only thing a philosopher has to do is to explain that disagreement of this sort occurs: to suggest what status the conflicting statements have: and to ensure that explanation is rid of the confusion which comes from supposing that he has to do anything more.

Nor are 'ends' a more suitable province for philosophical activity than 'means'. 'Ends' cannot in practice, without danger of paralysis, be separated from 'means', and ends that are pursued are everywhere affected by the means needed to attain them. Both have to be chosen: but the difficulties surrounding the act of choice require resolution in a particular time and place by all the agencies which determine the judgement of a particular society. Questions involving either can be resolved for that society alone, by those who have authority in it and by those who give advice in a practical and casuistical manner, about the relevance of the moral prejudices which emerge from its history, habits and religion. They are questions different in kind from questions presented to philosophers, who begin with the fact of moral judgement and the need to explain its nature and who are competent to say not whether certain actions are right or wrong but what is meant when men claim to know the difference. The political philosopher may, if he wants to, draw out the implications of the assumptions on which men around him act with a view, if he likes, to revealing their inconsistency with one another. He may also, if he feels inclined to, sneer at, satirize and ridicule the incoherences with which men deceive themselves in practice. But this, though flattering to his vanity, is not central to his calling. Inconsistency is no bar to action and may not be very much bar to right action either. All he can say, if he wishes to speak, is that if ideas which stimulate to action were used as a stimulus to explanation, explanation would be twisted.

Political philosophy, then, is concerned with the variation of opinions, with the fact that action need not be self-conscious in order to be rational or right and with the belief that we need not grasp the consequences of action in order to act rightly: and understanding of these things arises from realization of the contrast between intention and consequence, ideal and reality, what seems desirable and what is possible, Mind's ambition and its ability to control the world which lies at the heart of the human situation. Men, considering the world, see things that are bad, situations that are wrong, conditions that affront and feel compelled to reflect upon the source of anomalies which distress their natural desire to inhabit a world that yields to their own high standard of desirability. To halt life at a fixed point, to grasp pleasures that pass, to achieve relief from difficulties that press is a condition never wholly to be avoided. To grasp, also, remedies that are easy, courses that help and answers that make the world seem an agreeable place, displays only the strength, depth and pervasiveness of a contrast which cannot be explained away by seeing more clearly than we otherwise might the meaning of the words we tend to use. The impulse is there in all human activity: it is there in the effort, in political action, to imagine a world free from the problems inseparable from political existence.

The relevance of this should not be misunderstood. By some the contrast is treated as a challenge to be overcome by action designed in the world of practice to establish whatever men think it suitable to establish, whatever the difficulties in the way of establishing it.

For those who engage in political activity, this is a possible (if disillusioning) attitude with which it is not proposed to quarrel. Nor is it denied that books which advocate particular political actions have value, because books of this sort have consequences (sometimes even the consequences that are intended). Concern with this sort of consequence, however, is the function not of the philosopher but of the citizen or practical politician, and the validity of work of this sort with this sort of concern lies not in explanation but in action. Since, however, books of a reflective sort are written and since this is the activity to which attention is being drawn, we must ask what relevance they have. And the answer must be that, though they have only the most indirect connection with political practice, they are related to the situation of the philosopher and enable him to explain to himself the predicaments with which he is faced, the contrasts by which he is confronted and the limits within which his thought can be made effective. The world *looks* irrational, the creature of chance. It is an assumption, however, of the study we have in mind, that it yields something to rational consideration. It is the business of history to reveal as much of its rationality and regularity as it can and of philosophy to account for the fact that it gives the appearance of having neither. Political philosophy in this manner is related to the situation of the writer and gives guidance to him in his attempt to account for the limits of his power. Although it gives no guidance to political action, it gives guidance to thought, aid to explanation, assistance to seeing the world as clearly as it is. Political philosophy in this sense is thought not, as is sometimes suggested,[1] chiefly about thought but about action also: but not nevertheless, about action with a view to more action, but solely with

[1] D. M. MacKinnon, *A Study in Ethical Theory* (1957), pp. 204–5.

a view to better, clearer, more accurate, more adequate, more coherent thought. The only body of 'substantive political principles' which emerges from writing of this sort refers not to principles of action but to what may be called principles of thought. The only consequence that follows necessarily from thought of this sort is more thought and more interesting variations of it. The advice which comes refers not to questions like 'What is the just State?' and 'What ought to be done to bring it about?'; not 'What ought I to do in my present situation?'; not even 'Why should I pay my taxes or vote Labour?' but 'What is the best way of seeing things as they are: within what limits, and how, does the nature of political activity impose brakes upon a thinker's capacity to make effective his wishes for the world?' 'Substantive political principles', in this context, refer not to the conduct of political practice but to the conduct of political reflection: and although political philosophy is reflection about action, the continuum within which it occurs is one where explanation and understanding mark the limits and set the tone. The philosopher must assume a uniformity of explanatory concern which does not permit *him* to distinguish a good act from a bad one. Elsewhere this need not be so: if he is acting politically, he will have preferences (if arbitrary ones). So long as he is a philosopher, however, he must take all human activity as it comes, assuming that actions which have been widely condemned require explanation as much as actions which have not. Where preference or moral judgement is concerned he is, indeed, not so much neutral as totally indifferent: and although his preferences will almost certainly emerge in the course of his writing, his purpose as philosopher does not include an attempt to make them apparent. Political philosophy is not an impartial or disinterested activity: but its partiality and commitment are to a particular way of explaining the world, not to a particular line of political action. Praise and blame, anger and pleasure, conscientious belief and conscientious commitment are legitimate: but only so far as the explanations they give and the books they produce reveal the virtues or limitations of the explanatory tools philosophers are equipped with. This, no doubt, is a limiting conception of political philosophy. Limiting or not, it is a foundation for building which can be judged by the success with which philosophy, attempted on this basis, has been written in the past and can be written in the future; and not by the way in which the world is improved, political activity controlled or agreeable consequences achieved in practice.

Political philosophy, then, explains the limitations imposed by thought upon the thinker. And since the world it assumes to be rational and intelligible has the appearance of being arbitrary, unsatisfactory and disjointed, it is only by explaining its limitations that the first activity of philosophy can be accomplished. Its responsibility is not to its consequences in the world of action but to its consequences in the world of thought. The only criticism which consideration of consequences should imply of this sort of explanation, is not that it will subvert habits, damage society or destroy political stability, but that it will lead to blank ends in the line of thought. The tools with which this sort of explanation can be undertaken are numerous and the standard by which their utility can be judged does not yield to dismissal in advance of use. 'Metaphysics' has of late in some quarters come to mean any explanatory concept a particular philosopher does not find it helpful to employ: but it is best not to be dogmatic. Explanatory concepts like 'God', 'scale of being' or 'natural law' can be judged by their usefulness in practice in stimulating to explanatory writing. When phrases of this sort are used, meaning emerges not from restricting reference to the meanings of common speech but from the emphasis they are given in the tradition of thinking to which they belong. If to use them as explanatory tools seems to imply affiliation with particular religious commitments, no one need feel embarrassment. Few tools of this sort have origins which are exclusively philosophical: their philosophical value must in any case be measured by their use: and the usefulness of this set has been great.

It is, indeed, unnecessary to enquire in advance whether philosophical concepts are 'true': for we do not know whether they are or not. All we know is that they give exercise to certain sorts of mind. Their immediate value and relevance lie partly in the coherence with which they are expressed and partly in the intensity and intelligence with which they are manipulated. Explanation is the business of philosophy: explanation no less tentative and unsatisfactory than any other and giving no reason to claim greater certainty than it can yield. This is of importance so far as it affects the possibility of writing commonly called metaphysical and it may, therefore, be desirable to mention the objections which might be raised against the possibility of this sort of explanation of the nature of political judgement.

It is not to be supposed that the existence of works called 'metaphysical' is a justification for continuing to produce them. All may have been valueless, and contemporary suspicion a reassertion of common sense after a period of error and misunderstanding. Nevertheless, it may be that in the suspicion of metaphysics assumptions lie concealed which are self-destructive: and if any significant release is to be made from the scruples and strictness of those who are suspicious, it is necessary to persuade them that their own weapons and standards may be turned, not just against metaphysics but against the dogmatic certainty of those who claim that metaphysics is impossible. What is needed is to turn against their scruples, the scepticism of which they are exponents, and to persuade them (or their pupils) that, by their own standards, the activity of which they are the enemies has no less validity than the exact activity in which they engage.

A thoroughgoing scepticism here is important: for it is incompatible with the claim to *solve* philosophical problems not just in each generation but once and for all in a way which makes it unnecessary for them to be solved again. It makes nonsense of the certainty affected by any philosophical manner that its way (even if legitimate) is so much more legitimate than others that all others are illegitimate. It is incompatible, also, with the assumption that solutions which are reached have universal validity or express a truth which is true beyond reasonable doubt. In a tactical sense it is necessary, no doubt, that those who affect these certainties or teach this sort of subject should believe themselves to have reached the high peaks from which more can be seen than earlier philosophers could see before them. Also, it may well be the case that much contemporary suspicion, where moral and political writing is concerned, arises from a reaction against the absurd pretensions of ethical idealism—not just in providing incontrovertible truth but in deducing practical guidance from it. Nevertheless, along with the claim to avoid this particular error, goes the attribution of a perennial, incontrovertible certainty to a local style of explanation which induces in some contemporary philosophical writing a self-righteous pharisaism effectively destructive of the attempt to express whatever men think they know about reality by claiming for this local anti-metaphysic a certainty which no form of intellectual activity can achieve.

Philosophy does not elucidate truths more certain than those of any other sort of intellectual activity. Philosophy presents the world men know at a certain level of abstraction according to conventions which philosophers have built up over the generations and in which the use to which they are put is more important than the fundamental assumptions themselves. Philosophy does not in this respect differ from other academic disciplines. Philosophers ought not to suppose that the conventions of their own particular discipline approximate to a more certain truth than the conventions of another, or that the convention of any particular tradition of philosophical thinking can be known to be more true than any other. Truth is not the characteristic of an explanatory tool, which simply provides a starting-point for use. No academic subject has more than conventional validity: each shows what a number of generations can do with the particular tools they have to hand in organizing the subject-matter they have chosen to use them on with the intelligence and energy they have available. All are destined to be superseded by different tools and different conventions: and even if it may, for practical purposes, be necessary to believe otherwise, it is still as a matter of explanation the case. It is probable that in mid-Victorian Oxford the subject on which the greatest body of sustained intelligence worked would now be taught in faculties of divinity. The work which was produced displayed a toughness, subtlety and intellectual power equal to anything produced in philosophical faculties today. Professor Ryle is a powerful, subtle and lucid writer, but does not in his qualities surpass Newman. Professor Ayer's mind is no harder than Mansel and it cannot really be maintained that Professor Hampshire and Mr Warnock are, amongst more popular writers, greater than Liddon or Church. The vigour, combativeness and fertility of three generations of Oxford theologians produced a coherent apologetic which was validated less by the *truth* of its assumptions than by the intelligence with which they were treated. Its quality could in any case not be judged by judging the assumptions alone (which men are not generally free to choose) but only by considering the energy and intelligence displayed in dealing with them. Assumptions, like the ingredients of character, emerge as intellectual prejudices, nuggets of belief, by which intellectual activity is to be guided: and once a particular assumption has been questioned, another more fundamental replaces it. Although they are supposed by those who make them to be truths (which is to say that they are unable to question them), the philosopher finds that they are arbitrary commitments, postures which arise from the tradition in which a thinker thinks and having authority with him and others in it: but having no authority over anyone else.

The assumption with which we deal—that metaphysical explanation is irrelevant—may seem reasonable to those who have chosen or been taught to believe it. Since, however, it has no validity for those who have not, they need feel no obligation to it. The political philosopher need no more feel that the anti-metaphysical prejudice is a binding truth in political philosophy than the politician or citizen need feel commanded by the practical prejudices of political traditions different from his own. It is, indeed, only when assumptions are recognized for what they are that other prejudices may be displayed also, and only when scepticism about the competence of one set of prejudices to give a binding knowledge of reality is grasped that metaphysics becomes possible. So long as it is supposed that philosophy can give this sort of certainty, the impossibility of ultimate knowledge is likely to inhibit the inventiveness of those who attempt to give it. But only when it is seen that philosophy gives none of this certainty, and that many manners of explaining the world (provided they are subjected to the attention of sustained intelligence) may in time give as coherent accounts as the fruitfulness of the treatment permits, does it become possible to play the metaphysical game as little more than a game, with its own rules and prohibitions, its own insights, coherence and rewards without any pretence that it has any necessary claim to provide greater certainty than any other. No doubt in most activities it is better to arrive than to travel hopefully: but in philosophy it is not the arrival but the journey itself which matters. Philosophy provides no finality or absolute certainty. Only when this is understood does it seem sensible to offer up those sorts of explanatory activity which have exercised philosophers in the past, which exercise them in the present, and which may continue to exercise them in the future.

The obstacle in the path of metaphysics, in short, is not the claim of metaphysicians to know a greater reality than any other (though this may have been so once) but the tendency of those who criticize the attempt at metaphysics to expect it (and suspect it for failing to provide) a standard of verifiable truth which it is without the range of human understanding to supply. To say that a metaphysical assumption is unverifiable is irrelevant. Of course it is unverifiable. Equally, to say that it has no use in practice (except the practice of explanation) is irrelevant to the question under discussion. But that is no reason why each tradition of philosophical thinking should not say what it has to about reality (provided it is disciplined by self-criticism) and none whatever why meaning should be denied to thinkers who use God, Being, natural law or rational will as instruments of explanation instead of the verification principle or the paradigm case. Metaphysical writing is no more than one way of doing philosophy. It need not enquire beforehand whether its language has validity: its practitioners use it if they can in order to see what use it has. Metaphysical writing, no less than any other style of philosophy, helps to exercise minds. Every philosopher, whether he is transparent enough to admit this or not, makes metaphysical assumptions, and no explanation of the nature of political activity which pretends to be more than undiscriminating inventory can avoid them. The task of political philosophy is to make as transparent as possible the assumptions implicit in any way of speaking about politics: but that is all it can do and the affectation should be avoided of pretending that it can do more.

The metaphysical paradox is, therefore, that in metaphysics the certainties affected by those who engage in any particular form of practice are taken to have none of the certainty which has in practice to be imputed to them. When a politician decides that it is right to do this or that, it is reasonable, provided he has taken into account all the circumstances which to him seem relevant and made all the calculations which he supposes connect with the situation, in practice to say that he has done what he takes to be for the best—in other words, that he has done what he takes to be right. When a philosopher makes a contribution to philosophy, other philosophers will judge the sense, or stupidity, of the statement he has made. In all activities in which men engage minds that are at grips with their surroundings, know, if they are not mad, that they are, when they do anything, doing what they take to be the right thing at the right time in the right place: and the smaller the doubt they have about it, probably the better. Commitment to practice of this sort is an unavoidable facet of any man's situation in the world: and, though the degree varies to which individuals succeed in being relevant (or successful) enough to achieve competence in the area of practice in which they are engaged, no one except madmen (and even few madmen) escape the situations by which they are surrounded. In all forms of activity, men grow by practice, to a greater or lesser extent, into the conventions held relevant at the time and place in which they live. In doing so they edge convention—whether they intend to or not—in the direction in which they think it ought to go: and, even when they defy, thwart, denounce or disobey, they leave their mark upon the history of men's efforts to grapple with the difficulties of the world.

In all societies words are used to mark approval and disapproval, praise and blame, and in all activities the practical judgement involves commitment to the recurrent belief that good and bad, right and wrong, have self-evident meaning, to question the possibility of which is to contract out of serious consideration. If a lawyer offered as a ground for questioning a judge's judgement the fact that in a different legal system a different principle might be applied to determination of a particular case, then, whatever the relevance of his statement to philosophy, he would be thought to have abandoned his attempt at practice. In the English legal system a judge is taken to be reasoning about the question presented for judgement, and the fact that a judge might be under the impression that he is reasoning in a philosophical manner would neither alter the fact that he is not, nor reduce the practical usefulness of his judgement. A judge who has never heard of Professor Ayer will not, when reasoning in a judicial capacity, necessarily know that the reasons he gives in reaching his judgements might by some philosophers be thought arbitrary. He probably does not know, in any case he does not *need* to know, that anyone reflecting on them might well conclude that adoption in any particular society of one set of legal 'principles' rather than another must be thought of as the outcome of historical accident. All he knows is that he thinks his determination the 'right judgement in the circumstances' and in a practical context there is no reason why he should not. But if, in all other activities, practical certainty is appropriate, it is appropriate in philosophy only so far as the philosopher's function is to take the certainties apparent in these activities and ask what sort of certainty they are.

Nor can the paradox be resolved by suggesting that philosophy should subject words to analysis so searching that paradox in philosophy and misunderstanding in practice will be avoided as words come to be used more accurately in the future. To suppose so is to exaggerate the influence of an academic discipline. Lawyers and judges will exchange their certainties, historians, politicians and physicists will work with theirs: and they will do so whatever the philosopher may say about the adequacy of the language in which they do it. Those who engaged in practice did not await the analyses of Professor Popper before creating our civilization out of the past, and their descendants will act with whatever adequacy they can when Mr Hare is no longer with us in the future. Philosophers may, if they want to, attempt to determine in what ways language should be used in practice. But philosophers who do so will abandon the struggle with the central metaphysical problem—that what in practice seems necessary is not necessarily so, and that the philosopher's only obligation is to be so transparently sensitive in his use of language that he makes it clear that this problem is as important as it is.

History is not often supposed (except by Mr E. H. Carr) to have a normative function but that does not make it any less desirable to emphasize that it does not. The 'lessons of history', no less than the guidance of philosophy, are an illusion. If the business of philosophy is to clarify understanding of the nature of the commitments to which men are bound in practice, history in the area with which we are concerned shows nothing more than what historians take it that political activity is like. The function of historical writing is to order the world we see according to the assumption (as arbitrary as most practical assumptions are) that the world as it is has emerged from the past. Since all we have is what is left in the present, the past is something we assume. It is, however, not adequate just to say that historical writing is an attempt to describe how specific events occurred. Historical writing is, indeed, concerned with specific analysis or narrative: the use of generalization is to provide, in historian's shorthand, aids to explaining existing records in terms of the specific past from which they emerged. Nevertheless, when the full intelligence is writing at a level consonant with the subject-matter, explanation of the movement of each historical event reveals in a specific way something of the deviousness of the movement of events in general. Nor should it be supposed that it is the philosophy of history that is being admired. On the contrary. The philosophy of history is a grotesque mistake, the consequence of an attempt to impute to fortuitous accident the dignity of a divine or necessary purpose which in a philosophical context we assume to be hidden—a monumental error which imposes on the movement of the historical past as erroneous (and external) a necessity as contemporary political idolatry imputes to political events in the present. Whatever else may be admired, this particular error cannot.

However, if the intelligibility of the world is not to be discerned through the general movement of events, it is not to be supposed that the movement of history is unintelligible. It is, on the contrary, intelligible to those who examine it when they have the skill, energy and luck to gear their intelligence to an intelligible subject-matter; and so far as they recognize that the limit of intelligibility is reached when the intentions of actors in the past (which are themselves in principle wholly intelligible) begin to conflict with one another. Conflict is fortuitous: is not the work of mind: and is therefore in some sense unexpected. Though fortuitous, however, and unexpected, it is nevertheless specific, discernible and intelligible. But intelligible fact does not reveal itself in general, only in particular: and if intelligibility is to be exposed at all, it is necessary for the philosophic historian to study in a specific way the central evidence for the study he is making. Historical writing, like philosophical writing, is explanation validated by the assumption that thought, disciplined by the coherence of a tradition of thinking, is capable of making intelligible the subject-matter on which it works, and that the explanation (narrative or analytical) given in any historical work can within limits be verified by other historians who repeat the experiment of looking at the documents under discussion. The only sense in which one may speak of a science of history is the sense in which verificatory conventions are used by professional historians who know roughly, and agree roughly, about the way in which they are to be applied. The standard of verification is rough: the 'experiment' can be said to be 'controlled' only because the historian can both decide what to look for in the documents and can read them with a hypothesis in mind about what they will produce. But that historical explanation is conducted according to conventions in important respects the same as those that operate in the natural sciences—the conventions of explanatory hypothesis, experimental verification and confirmation or modification—should not, whatever the difference in the sort of statement that is aimed at, be doubted.

Historians, of course, have no assurance that the past was as they think it was (for the past is no longer with us). It is not the events from the past which present themselves for explanation, but only the relics in the present. The events of the past are things the historian constructs: and although many historians suppose they are explaining the past, all they have is a rough idea of the way events can occur and the dead documents that speak, to validate or disprove their hypotheses. In historical (as in all other) activity there is the possibility of error, nonsense and futility; and to avoid the attempt merely because certainty is impossible is to be inhibited by an immaculateness so overwhelming that nothing will ever be accomplished. The subject-matter of history is the buildings, letters, documents and remains existing today and demanding explanation from those who choose to give it. The buildings, letters, documents and remains are specific objects, not general ones: they suggest specific pasts, not generalized ones, and, although every explanation suggests a general conception of the way in which events occur, they yield their share of response to the explanatory intelligence only so far as they are approached in a specific manner.

This means that for the purpose we have in mind historical writing is unlikely to be illuminating unless a large body of subject-matter is available on which the explanatory intelligence can work. It means also that the greatest danger in the way of historical understanding is half-information, evidence that tells us something like the thing we want to know but not the thing itself. To know, for example, that the Cabinet supported the appointment of Mr Macmillan as Prime Minister is to know a single fact: but it throws no light upon the way in which the appointment was brought about. To know that Mr Khrushchev attacked President Eisenhower at the Summit Conference in Geneva in 1960 is to know something: but it is to know nothing of any great consequence for the present study. To know the names of the permanent under-secretaries of British ministries and to have a generalized account of their formal relationship with each other is to have a still-life picture of the structure of government. But still-life pictures of Mr Macmillan's appointment, Mr Khrushchev's speech and the public and formal relations between government departments, though useful facts on which to build, very often conceal (and are sometimes intended to conceal) rather than of explain, the way in which events occur.

In the various sorts of historical writing varying sorts of evidence are desirable. Not all sorts of historical writing have reached the same stage of development. In economic history the intelligibility of the subject-matter will be revealed not, as seems sometimes to have been thought at a primitive stage in the development of the subject, by studying the writings of economic theorists, but by studying a wider, and less deliberately articulate, body of evidence. If the subject were the history of economic thought, Adam Smith's opinions would be of primary importance. But in economic history, the subject-matter for explanation is the hedges and ditches, houses and dykes, fens and roads which leave their marks on the English landscape, and the factories, cities, railways and offices, and the documents in firms, government departments and country houses which invite consideration. The opinions of Adam Smith, so far as they affected the growth of English industry in the nineteenth century, were important: but at least as important are the intentions and achievements of the thousands of men who had by 1850 made England the richest country in the world. Unfortunately, much of what is wanted cannot be discovered. The records of firms are not as detailed as the records of government and many questions which deserve answers cannot really be asked. Whereas in diplomatic and political history the articulateness of the actors makes it possible to discern the conflicts which we assume to exist everywhere between intention and consequence, interpretation of reality and the reality itself, in economic history this is not often possible and it is conceivable that over large stretches it may not be possible at all.

Just as philosophical explanation is subject to the assumptions of philosophers and physics to the assumptions of physicists (which are not necessarily drawn from the subject-matter on which they work), so historical explanation is subject to the character and assumptions of historians. Since historians have only letters, buildings and pictures from the past and not the living men themselves, explanation varies according to the character, intelligence and shape of mind of the historian himself. This is neither deplorable nor surprising. The more fertile and promising the subject-matter, the greater the historian's opportunity to display the range of his understanding of the motives and connections which constitute historical events. What gives historians the opportunity to contribute to political explanation is not the chronological accident that a period dealt with is recent and therefore 'political': or that it reveals the structure of 'contemporary', as distinct from 'historical', society: but the challenge presented to high intelligence and intensity of thought to make the best of a fruitful subject-matter, whatever the period.

It may in passing be added that economic theory must in this respect be treated as a form of explanation without authority in practice. Where it is not in fact a loosely generalized version of some piece of specific historical explanation, economic theory has authority to push to the limit of theoretical possibility the factors isolated by economists in order to establish possible correlations between whatever variables the economist has chosen to consider. Statements in economic theory often have *consequences* in practice but they have *authority* only within the framework of the explanatory construct. Theoretical statements which *look* relevant to practice, which are indeed used in practice, are in reality models of ideal situations which there is no reason to suppose have any necessary relationship to the problems which confront those who make practical decisions. Nor is it relevant to criticize economic theory for being theoretical. The 'art of political economy'—the application of economic theory to economic practice—is by its very nature a practical, and not an explanatory, activity. It may have consequences for economic theory when its problems suggest ways in which the subject could be developed: but any other intellectual activity may also. Explanatory economics is, in much the same way as mathematics, a world of theoretical constructions in which hypotheses are pushed as far as the energy of the thinker can push them. Conflict and consensus are as likely there as in any other academic discipline. But to regret failure to gear this irresponsible intellectual game to the problems confronting Chancellors of the Exchequer or Company chairmen is to be guilty of a serious confusion.

Behind every economic decision taken in board rooms or government departments, there are many factors as relevant as the economic doctrines to which the decision-maker has become committed: and even if those who have to make decisions could see the economic problem as clearly as they would like, they would still not be able to act as suitably (or necessarily as successfully) as they could wish to. Given a particular account of the reasons for slump and boom, employment and unemployment in a particular country at a particular time and given general agreement amongst economists about them, those who have responsibility to make political decisions would still be free not just (as when there is disagreement amongst economists) to decide which economist to prefer, but, if they chose to, to doubt their predictions altogether. Economic theory is a body of explanation: and economists, as economists, have no more right to regard their doctrines as commands to action than historians, philosophers or anyone else.

Economists, of course, frequently do claim for their study more than a purely explanatory function. Sir Dennis Robertson imputes to 'the study of economics . . . the formation of judgements, which one can bring to bear according to one's opportunities—as employer, as civil servant, as minister of religion, or just as ordinary citizen and voter—on proposals for the promotion of human welfare . . . some, though by no means all of which . . . involve political action'.[1] In reply to the question 'if and so far as the objective of high employment is being given primacy [in any particular country], are we to say that one sort of economic welfare is being sacrificed to another . . . or that economic welfare in general is being curtailed for a non-economic end?', he answers that, 'in situations of this kind the economist has a special duty to act as watchdog for economic welfare in the narrower sense in which it depends on high efficiency and high

[1] Sir Dennis Robertson, *Lectures on Economic Principles* (1957), vol. I, p. 17.

output, since if *he* doesn't nobody else will!!'[1] Again, in estimating the part national power and national strength should play in the increase of general welfare, the economist is, in Sir Dennis's view, under a 'special duty to think and act as a watchdog for welfare in a sense of that word which is less than co-extensive with *all* the aims which are set up as goals for human behaviour'.[2]

There could be no objection to this formulation of the economist's function if Sir Dennis's concern for welfare were really an explanatory one; if, that is to say, he were attempting to explain in what sort of circumstances certain sorts of satisfaction or efficiency (neutrally defined) had in the past been obtained. Nor would there be objection to his account of the scope of *Ethics* and *Politics* if he meant what he said when he described them as 'the study of how people *think* [my italic] they ought to behave, both as individuals and as members or officers of organized communities'.[3] Unfortunately, it is clear that he means, on the contrary, that ethics and politics may enjoin one set of actions and economics another: and that, in these circumstances, 'the economist must be prepared to see some suggested course of action which he thinks would promote economic welfare turned down . . . on the ground, as in the case for instance of the removal of a protective duty on steel, that it would impair national security'. If, of course, the overriding economic injunction is taken always to be 'increased efficiency' or 'increased productivity', then the conflict between *Politics* and *Economics* is a real one. If, also, it is taken to have some other meaning (productivity, perhaps, combined with lowering of prices), the conflict would still exist—with a different content. But since it is impossible, in real situations, to isolate the economic element in welfare (because in practice all elements in action are

[1] Robertson, p. 20.   [2] Robertson, p. 21.   [3] Robertson, p. 29.

connected) and since it is arbitrary to assume that 'efficiency in production' is a more 'economic' motive than, say, 'providing employment as widely as possible'; since, in short, the objects of 'economic' action, like the objects of 'good' action are amongst men heterogeneous, there is no academic point in attempting to give practical advice which can be confronted by the mere expression of a contrary prejudice. All the academic economist has authority to do is to juggle with the variables with which he is concerned in order to explain, not that welfare should be maximized, but that maximization (conceived in this way or that) tends to occur as certain economic variables take effect.

Sir Dennis's position is also the position implied in Mrs Joan Robinson's claim that 'the element of propaganda is inherent [in economics] because it is concerned with policy', in her assertion that 'it would be of no interest if it were not' and in the belief that 'if you want a subject that is worth pursuing for its intrinsic appeal without any view to consequences you would not be attending a lecture on economics . . . [but doing] pure mathematics or studying the behaviour of birds'.[1] It is certainly true that 'Economics' ought to be concerned with 'policy' and 'consequences': but only because it is concerned to understand them. No doubt every economist, like every historian, reveals his preferences in developing an attitude to the subject-matter with which he is dealing: and Mrs Robinson is right to discern in Marx, Marshall and Keynes political impregnations which show them, severally, attempting 'to understand the [capitalist] system in order to hasten its overthrow', 'to make it acceptable by showing it in an agreeable light' and 'to find out what has gone wrong . . . in order to devise means to save it from destroying itself'.[2] No

[1] J. Robinson, *Collected Economic Papers*, vol. II, p. 4. [2] Robinson, p. 1.

reader of these writers would question these brief charac-
terizations. Nevertheless, no one (and not, it is evident,
Mrs Robinson)[1] would suppose that Marx's, Marshall's
or Keynes's explanations of the nature of capitalist
economic activity could be defended or attacked, merely
by describing the differing judgements each makes of
the desirability of the system they describe. Once inadequacy is discerned in an economist's analysis, the
extraneous political purposes to which he is committed
might be relevant in accounting for it. But to uncover
the origin of a style of explanation (an origin which, in
complicated minds, is likely to be complicated) does
nothing to confirm, or confute, its adequacy. It is not
impossible for a Marxist economist substantially to agree
(as indeed many do) with non-Marxists about the
characteristics of wide areas of economic activity. Nor,
so long as there is a body of explanatory writing and a
wide range of explanatory concern, is it impossible to
confine the academic authority of economic statements
within an explanatory field of reference. The fact that
economists may be in demand in government (as theologians were once and as Sir Charles Snow would like
scientists to be in the future) has no more significance
for the academic study of economics than the appear-
ances of bird-watchers on television have for academic
ornithology. What each generation of academic economists thinks worth explaining will vary according (among
many other things) to the political interests and political
preferences of each: but, even if total agreement is never
likely, that is no reason why the conventions of the subject-matter should not produce a certain measure of
professional agreement about some of the questions under
discussion. It may have been a desire to see capitalism

[1] Cf., 'it is folly to reject a piece of analysis because we do not agree with the
political judgement of the economist who puts it forward', p. 6.

destroyed which made Marx expect working-class wages to decline or it may have been because he thought working-class wages were declining that Marx wanted to see capitalism destroyed. In disentangling motive and motivation of this sort, caution is desirable. But what is quite certain is that once it has been decided which questions are worth asking, it is possible (within the limits allowed by the indeterminacy of the subject-matter) to say what correlations exist between the economic variables under consideration—and that this may in some cases be done whatever an economist's political prejudice makes him *want* to believe. As Mrs Robinson rightly observes, 'an economic theory is at best only an hypothesis . . . suggests a possible explanation of some phenomenon and . . . cannot be accepted as correct until it has been tested by an appeal to the facts': though this, one must add, applies equally to the constructions of historians and the hypotheses of ornithologists—because it is characteristic of all bodies of explanation.

Theological writing, on the other hand, is almost always part of practical activity and designed with a view to action. The 'philosophy of religion' is not a branch of theology and cannot give greater authority to theological statements than they themselves in practice can command. Since the philosophy of religion is the work which is produced when philosophers attempt to explain what theological statements are for, it has relevance for philosophical explanation alone. But, although in philosophy it is assumed that we do not know that our explanations do justice to the reality they affect to explain, in theological writing it is thought necessary to assume that they do. There are occasions on which theologians can allow themselves the luxury of doubt: but doubt, extensively entertained, will not maintain effective testimony to a living God. To propagate a revelation that is for all *practical* purposes true (if that does not beg the questions) is the fundamental appeal and starting-point of any religion. Its chief practical purpose is to offer the possibility of salvation to men and women of all degrees of explanatory competence, and this cannot be other than a practical activity. Salvation comes not just by getting one's explanations right (though to get them as right as one can, no doubt, helps): and if the pursuit of philosophical transparency makes it more difficult to achieve, then, even in the most intelligent of religions, salvation will come first. Salvation comes from the whole of the response men make to their lives: and account is no doubt taken in God's Judgement, the natural law, the scale of being or whatever absolutely substantive ground the universe is supposed to have, of the opportunities offered, and the opportunities taken, in the attempts an individual makes to pursue it.

In explanation one may say this: but it is doubtful whether one may say very much else. Those who propagate religions have renounced the academic task of explaining everything and enjoining nothing. On the contrary, even when they know that it limits their adequacy in explanation, they are concerned with action —and with nothing else. It does not matter whether the religion is the religion of Christianity or the religion of Enlightenment: nor is the relevance of this statement affected by the fact the high explanatory attention is devoted in nearly all religions to establishing the meaning of ancient texts. In Europe almost all academic explanation has grown up within the framework, and to serve the needs, of one religion or the other. In religion, authorities command, lay claim to revelation, speak in an apparently explanatory manner about the truths of propositions concerning the nature of the world, and are attended to as though their statements have explanatory authority. But though not, for this reason, less important in practice, these statements are explanatory in appearance only: they do not just say what is the case or explain the character of their own internal logic. On the contrary, in a world where explanatory activity leads only to recognizing the impossibility of using explanatory tools to decide which view to assent to, their chief function is to hold together the innumerable seekers after salvation by facilitating bold, inflexible choices, which may or may not be wrong (in God's eyes): which may be irrelevant to his purposes; but which though arbitrary, are the only communal resource available to those who wish to assist in accomplishing them. That they are arbitrary (and not necessarily the consequence of understanding God's word) cannot in practice be admitted by their exponents. That they are not, in explanation, statements of this sort implies nothing about their usefulness in practice. They are in fact all men have in the world of practice to which all belong: and, if they cannot certainly be said in explanation to achieve the comprehensiveness they claim, the ultimate judgement may nevertheless take account of the fact that arbitrariness is necessary to the function they perform.

The function of moral theology is to keep the practical judgement in repair, and since this is a practical task, its bases, though arbitrary, must be definitive. It is not adequate in practice to say that all human effort is equidistant from God (or that we cannot judge the distances). Even though we do not know, we have in practice still to judge, whilst in explanation pursuing the implications of the fact that our judgement is fallible. And if, with Professor Coulson for example,[1] it be implied that this sort of ignorant human understanding cannot be the work

---

[1] *Science and Christian Belief* (1955), p. 21.

of a reasonable God, one may answer that, if the possibility can be conceived that God wishes to test Man's intelligence by so limiting its capacity that a serious temptation arises from the tendency to ignore these limitations, then a deficiency in reasonableness is no bar to his having done so. What content should one give to the phrase 'reasonable God' or 'God for whom Professor Coulson has some use'? If a 'reasonable' God has made the universe as deviously discernible as he may have done, then he may well display his reasonableness by making the act of knowing more interesting than it might otherwise be. It may be that it is not *what* is known that is necessary to understanding: but that what is known should be known in such a way that we do not suppose ourselves to know more than we do. And if this is a condition of human understanding and a necessary part of thought, then, even if the God who made the world may be a sophisticated God, He should not necessarily be thought an unreasonable one.

If the philosophy of religion is not part of theology, nor should jurisprudence be thought to contribute anything to the literature of law. Jurisprudence is part of explanatory philosophy—the part in which philosophers explain what status legal actions and legal statements have. Jurisprudence is not, as is sometimes supposed, the enunciation of general principles to which laws ought to conform (for that is a part of legislative practice in which philosophers have no particular authority). Jurisprudence, like any other academic activity, has no normative authority. What philosophers say about the nature of law and the character of legal statements may well impinge, deviously and indirectly, on the practice of lawyers: but the only purpose with which the student of jurisprudence has any obligation to be concerned is to see as clearly as he can the nature of the activity to which his attention has been turned. There is, of course, a legal literature of the first practical consequence which explains, for the benefit of lawyers and legislators, what the existing law must be taken to be. Apart from (usually inadequate) prefatory attempts to consider the status of the statements made in the body of these works, the best of them enunciate 'legal principles', illustrate them by reference to cases in the past and suggest, in anticipation of cases in the future, what judges or juries may be expected to decide about questions which will, for purposes of decision, be thought similar. The importance of these works cannot be exaggerated. Though often without formal standing, they constitute a body of influential rules which set the framework within which advocates and judges do their work. They are not supposed to do more than record, and an important function of an advocate is to apply the law-book's general principle to the circumstances of his client. In a legal system, however, where much depends on argument and precedent (and often on precedent established three or four centuries ago), the importance of legal teaching and law text-books in shaping the minds of lawyers and defining practical principles is great. Nevertheless, there are certain things that writers of legal text-books are not concerned to do. They do not, for example, explain a law or decision 'historically'. The context in which a decision was made, or a statute enacted, in the past is, to any but a limited degree, indifferent to the writer of a legal text-book. It may sometimes be necessary, in order to understand the purpose of a statute or judicial decision, to ask what it was designed (by Parliament, for example) to do: but this is not always necessary and the level of historical explanation is likely to be low. No historian would take public ministerial statements as adequate explanation of a government's intentions, though lawyers, for legal purposes, frequently think it adequate to do so. All a law text-book will supply (and all it will be intended to supply) will be a statement of the principles on which it has hitherto been taken that cases should be decided in the English courts. Precision of statement will vary according to the number of cases taken into consideration and the comprehensiveness of the legislation under discussion: and also, no doubt, according to the competence of the writer: but it will not necessarily be improved because a writer has strong views about the virtues, or limitations, of the existing system. The law text-books show what the law is because the law text-book writer knows what conventions prevail with regard to the admissibility of laws and decisions: though he may, where no authoritative decision has been made, himself be, and leave his readers, in a condition of uncertainty about what judges will in future take it that the law is meant to be.

Even if, when energetic or opinionated, a law text-book writer points out that a judge, in a particular case, by failing to follow the precedents, seems to have contravened the principle that emerges from them, he has no authority to say, as Dr Glanville Williams, for example, says, that 'the decision . . . [in Dadson's case] . . . is wrong'.[1] The rightness or wrongness of a judicial decision can be determined by a higher court and by no one else. The legal text-book writer has authority to perform a positive task, not a normative one, to record what, so far as it can be known, the law is; to assume (and sometimes explicitly to argue) the nature of the rules by which it is declared in order to explain (with a high degree of probability) what the law may be expected to be tomorrow. The principles which are enunciated, though they seem reasonable to lawyers, must in any

---

[1] G. Williams, *The Criminal Law* (ed. 1953), p. 25.

sort of reflective explanation be thought arbitrary. Dr Glanville Williams tells us that 'it is not enough to create criminal responsibility that there are *mens rea* and an act: the actus must be *reus*' and that 'if I carry off my own umbrella thinking that I am stealing somebody else's, there are the *mens rea* of larceny and an act but not the *actus reus* of larceny'.[1] When he says this, he is telling us what he takes to be a fundamental principle of the system he is describing (which is, as it happens, the English system); and we may take it that he is right. Yet it is not just a linguistic quibble to suggest that a different legal principle, by attaching criminal responsibility to the act of 'carrying off my own umbrella thinking that I am stealing someone else's' could be accepted as part of a rule of law quite as much as the principle which is accepted in England now. In speaking of the 'rule of law', it matters very little *what* principles are taken to be fundamental, so long as the system in which they are developed has procedural regularities (the exact character of which varies from society to society) and so long as those who operate, and those who are subject to, them feel no unbearable strain in making them work. The absence of a 'rule of law' can be attested only by those who are involved in any particular social structure. Only those who, because they are confined within the tradition itself, have a working knowledge of the nuances which any highly developed system displays are in any position to judge the rationality and reasonableness of a judgement or the suitability of a decision which has been made in the past or is likely to be made in the future. In any particular legal system the words 'reasonable', 'rational', 'probable' and 'common sense' come over the years to be given determinate content: but it cannot be said that the content they get is a necessary one. As

---

[1] Williams, p. 16.

Dr Williams observes 'In a philosophical view nothing is certain . . . so-called certainty is merely high probability . . . we do in fact speak of certainty in ordinary life: and for the purpose of the present rule it means such a high degree of probability that commonsense could pronounce it certain'.[1] One may agree with this, so long as it is understood that 'common sense' means in the English system no more than 'what a judge or jury are persuaded to accept as the judgement of common sense'. What seems the 'judgement of common sense' to one set of people, however, will not necessarily seem so to another. Dr Williams considers the situation in which 'the responsible officers of a railway company . . . [knowing] that by causing trains to run at sixty miles an hour, there is some risk of causing injury to passengers— more risk than if all trains were run at slower speeds, [yet] decide to incur it'.[2] He observes that 'on the whole the hazard is too small to be taken into account by a reasonable man', that 'as a community we prefer speed to safety to a certain extent' and that 'there is, therefore, no recklessness for legal purposes'. As to the fact that in our own society judges will share his views about the relationship between 'speed' and 'safety' he is right. This, however, is not to say, and nor does Dr Glanville Williams suppose, that it is *necessary* that they should think this way, or that in another society (or in our own a hundred and fifty years ago) other judges might not have decided differently—and with equal authority. It is possible to conceive of a legal system in which reasonable men would judge sixty miles an hour an unreasonable speed or where the mere execution of an act would be sufficient to create criminal responsibility. What gives authority to Dr Williams's enunciation of contrary principles is that since, over the centuries, in English legal

<hr>

[1] Williams, pp. 36–7.   [2] Williams, p. 52.

practice lawyers have come to use them as fundamental assumptions of the English law, they are binding now on those who wish to take part in English justice. English justice is what happens to be given in the English courts: including whatever process of suit and judgement is determined by the prevailing authority according to whatever principles that authority happens to follow. In this sense one may say that the content of law is arbitrary, that it is what those who exercise authority in any society have decided; and that, whatever may be thought about the rightness or wrongness of any particular laws or the procedures by which justice is administered, the law in any particular society at any particular time on any particular question which calls for determination is what those who have authority decide it is, and nothing else.

Nor is the status of psychological writing much different from that of jurisprudence. There is in this field, on the one hand, a body of psychological explanation of the nature of the mental process and of relations between the individual and society which has serious explanatory significance. And there is, on the other hand, a body of writing designed to give guidance to psychological therapy which constitutes the professional equipment of the practising psychologist. These practical principles are not comprehensive explanations of the nature of the mind, but guides to action, suggestions about the sort of steps which may be taken to alleviate a distressing mental condition. 'Sufficient practical knowledge' of this kind is given in the teaching hospitals and university medical schools. It need not be identical with the explanation given to each other by academic specialists: though between the practitioner and the academic psychologist, a considerable traffic is likely as prevailing theoretical constructs are modified, or discarded, by those who find them unhelpful in practice.

In this connection it is necessary to be clear about three things. In the first place practical psychology has hardly any authority in political practice. It is true that the law courts are increasingly compelled, as Parliament has increasingly chosen, to take account of psychological advice in determining the nature and scale of punishment for crime: but determination of the limits of sanity and determination of punishment for crime (though affected by the state of psychological explanation) remain at the discretion of judges and juries. 'Sanity', like 'sensible', is a word without necessary content: the content it gets is given by whoever has authority to give it, and authority, in the English courts, is not in the hands of psychologists. Secondly, psychological explanation has no *necessary* relevance to political practice. In determining what 'normal' or 'insane' is going to mean, academic psychologists will have whatever authority legal laymen allow them: but, if the *practising* psychologist cannot necessarily expect his judgements to be accepted by the courts, there is no reason why the academic psychologist should either. And if they do, they will do so for no reason more *necessary* than that psychology, like any other academic subject, has *some* effect on the general climate of opinion and because, occasionally, politicians come to office who happen to be interested in the views of its exponents. Nor need anyone who engages in political (or any other sort of) action feel any sort of inhibition in taking whatever action he wishes to take because a greatly extended understanding of the nature of human motivation suggests that what he supposes to be his motive might not in explanation be taken to be his real motive at all. If a particular psychological hypothesis about the nature of political motivation is attractive, it will play its part in the picture each generation has of the nature of political action, and may in this way affect the political climate. Explanatory psychological insight is, however, not a necessary preliminary to right political action, which may be taken in psychological ignorance as well. Finally, there is psychological explanation itself which becomes, at a certain point, an integral part of philosophical explanation. The point at which ostensible motives are said to conceal real motives, the transparency which occurs when glimpses are given of the complication and deviousness with which all human motivation is surrounded and the account given by social psychology of the relationship between men, their families and their social surroundings should be central to the concern of all adequate political philosophers. This is not to say that the explanatory tools used by psychologists will necessarily be useful to the philosopher. The explanatory tools of psychological study arise from the practical psychological function and have therefore to be scrutinized for signs of the arbitrariness to which such tools are subject. Nor will psychology command attention longer than the intelligence of psychologists merits. Formal social psychology has, of late in this country, contributed hardly anything of consequence to these enquiries. Nevertheless, whatever the limitations of existing studies in England, specific investigation of the specific subject-matter—the nature of a human mind —with whatever explanatory tools a psychologist wants to employ, is of first relevance to the study we are describing.

A word finally may be said about sociology, not in relation to its acceptability as an undergraduate subject in English universities (where a certain difficulty, a clearly academic intention and a relevant literature are the only important prerequisites) but because it is relevant to the questions under discussion. Its relevance is not, however, as specific as is sometimes suggested. As the argument of this book has indicated, if any British sociologist accepts the claim that sociology has a normative function in relation to social policy, then the claim he is accepting is illegitimate. Sociologists have no business to be establishing the content of 'rational policy or a rational ethic', and if they do, they have ceased to perform the academic function. Nor is it a function of sociology to do what is sometimes called 'unifying the social sciences'. 'Unification' is not a process to which any of the separate subject-matters needs to be subjected. A science is a body of explanation and nothing more: and nothing more is capable of explanation than the specific subject-matter with which it deals. Each of the sciences explains the subject-matter to which attention has been turned and explanation of the evidences of what men do in social and political action is a subject-matter of the greatest diversity. 'Unifying' generalization is a secondary abstraction from the act of explanation itself. Its validity, and only use, is to suggest to those who want them, ways of approaching whatever subject-matter is under discussion. There is, in the social sciences as everywhere else, a tension between the range of explanation indicated by the intellectual climate in which scholars live and the willingness of the subject-matter to provide evidence that they are right. There are occasions when unifying generalization (however illegitimate its intention) provides a stimulus to detailed explanation, but there are occasions also on which it does not. The opinions of a generation, uncritically applied to a subject-matter which cannot prove what that particular generation wants it to, make nonsense of the pretension to 'scientific method'. Even in the hands of scholars who are aware of the difficulties, interpretation can never be definitive. Weber's generalization about Calvinism and Capitalism formed exploratory bases for more than one generation of scholars: and yet it cannot be said that the story is told or discussion ended. Namierite accounts of the nature of political motivation were worked out on a period of English history which had attracted extensive attention in the century before Sir Lewis Namier was born. Sir Lewis was energetic and intelligent, but one cannot say that his range of reference provides a comprehensive account of the factors which moved men politically between the fall of Walpole and the loss of the American colonies. And if this is true where attempts can be made to understand the 'élite' under discussion (because evidence is available), it is even more likely to be true where the central subject-matter is missing. The idea seems at times to be abroad that political sociology can in some way unify political studies by extending the prevailing range of explanation. Yet, if one looks at what politico-sociological writing *is*, it seems either to be concerned with voting behaviour (which has relevance to the logic of chance but is only marginal to the central functions of government) or to expose a range of assumptions about the functioning of élites without even the range of evidence available to historians of eighteenth-century England. This point has been made already in relation to political science but (since no distinction exists except in the minds of some academic appointments committees) it may be said equally of political sociology. The literature of 'élites', like the pressure-group literature, wants a necessary dimension, not because the varying ideas about the influence of élites are wrong and not because they are unimportant, but because it is impossible to establish by reference to the material available any conclusion of importance. Verification might be possible if the 'élite' were candid: if, that is to say, it exposed its intentions to the public. The 'élite', however, in Britain, is not candid and unless it becomes so, sociological insights will be crude. Explanation needs as detailed a subject-matter as can be found and unification which abridges the detailed elaboration is unlikely to be fruitful. The only unity between the social sciences is the unity which comes as scholars turn their attention to the subjects under consideration in order to surround each with the same sort of explanation as they give to others. This is all that can be expected: to *expect* more will resolve none of the difficulties such expectations involve.

If the normative and unifying functions of sociology are rejected, what, then, is left? Very little, it is suggested, which is not embraceable within the field of historical study and explicable in terms of historical explanation. Sociology has no distinctive subject-matter. It is a short-hand term to describe particular ways of approaching particular subject-matters. Sociologists may claim that their peculiar province is 'social uniformities and social interrelations' but these problems are central to the work of historians, economists and anthropologists also. No doubt there are occasions when sociologists have ground to complain about the arrogance of historians and no doubt historians could sometimes learn something from sociological theory. Sometimes, perhaps, historical writing on any particular period would gain from intellectual infusions of the range and intelligence of Schumpeter. Nevertheless, whatever by-products they produce, sociological statements are aids to explanation and nothing more, and where political sociology is concerned, the chief manner in which they can be used is an historical one. Social anthropology does not tell us what primitive peoples do but what a primitive people does (or did when a scholar went to see it). Sociologists of advanced societies do not tell us 'how advanced societies conduct their affairs' but how certain facets of their affairs (usually the political or family arrangements) operate in specific instances of which the sociologist has experience. If anything more general is said, the generalization is a hint to further elucidation of the subject-matter and to nothing more: and, however complicated the language in which it is expressed, it is historical explanation and nothing else.

Nor does generality and abstraction resolve the problem with which all historical explanation is faced—of finding a subject-matter fruitful enough to demonstrate the variety and deviousness of human action. Of political sociology, as of all other political explanation, one may say that the political periods most likely to yield serious explanation are periods when reticence no longer envelopes the élite—periods, that is to say, when the passage of time and availability of evidence make it possible to come to grips, not just with the fact that an élite existed but also with the problems presented by the fact that a gap divided what it thought it was doing from what in fact it did. A political subject-matter needs to be surrounded with every sort of explanation: but it is necessary first to have a subject-matter to surround. Many facets of late-Victorian political life must now for ever elude the historian. About many facets of contemporary English politics, however, we know, and must for some time be content to know, even less. In matters of this sort dogmatism is undesirable: but much may be said for the view that political sociology will flourish best by turning attention to the innumerable questions which are still unanswered about the power, habits and intentions of the British political élite of the day before yesterday.

If, then, these various disciplines which together constitute a body of political explanation, provide no body of commanding political principle, what do they supply? And if they do not supply this, what does supply it? To answer the second question will lead to answering the first. For the substantive political principles for which the search goes on emerge for most men, not from the writings of philosophers but from political activity itself. Churches and States, groups and institutions, the laws positive and the beliefs which arise in a particular society —all between them provide for each generation its own embodiment of some of the guides to what it conceives it right to do. These rights are temporary and conventional, and they are nothing more. They cannot be known to be ultimate truths or eternal principles. They do not demonstrate, in unequivocal form, anything resembling the eternal law. All they provide is the nearest men can get with the tools they have inherited to what they think they ought to do. Nothing more can be expected: to expect more is to invite confusion. Political principles are not commands which bind all men in all places, but what each man or society thinks binding in a particular time and place. Each has been committed to a particular course of action, to defend or assault particular institutions and advocate particular causes, and will not be deflected by violence, bribery or persuasion. What is meant is that a man or a society has chosen to believe that, amongst all the courses which could be followed, one rather than another is of an importance which justifies overriding the claims of other men and other societies, and even their own more immediate interests. This, so far from flowing from philosophy, is an aspect of the operation of the practical judgement. The practical judgement alone tells whether the course of action proposed is possible: the practical judgement alone judges desirability: and the practical judgement draws its standard from judgement of preference as situations arise in the passing world. To live thus is to live in no condition of amorality, but to live in as close conformity to the moral law as possible. To think (or live) otherwise, if it is possible at all, is to be guilty of a moralistic irrelevance destructive of the power of thought. But if no body of substantive political principle exists in isolation from the actions through which it is embodied, what political function does political philosophy perform? Does it, indeed, perform any except to warn those who have been insufficiently insulated against irresponsible thought that reflective thought is best confined within its limits: that its only relevance is to make clear these limits and render more coherent than it has been in the past that body of explanation about the nature of political activity of which the historical and philosophical modes are the only serious constituents?

III

IT MIGHT towards the end of a work of this sort seem desirable to say what the author himself supposes 'freedom', 'goodness', or 'rationality' to imply in relation to existing policies in existing society: to indicate what he takes to be the urgent problems of our time: and suggest practical commitments which will make it possible to resolve them in the future. Precedents are not wanting for confining the application of methodological warnings to criticism of the work of others. However, if the argument of this work means anything, it means that declarations of this sort are irrelevant to the academic concern: and, since this is offered as a contribution to academic study, the temptation will be resisted. No attempt will be made to decide in what direction 'democratic principle' requires restriction to be placed on the freedom with which political parties buy public relations advice: no suggestion will be made about the extent to which the 'principle of equality' implies modification of existing arrangements regarding access to public schools: and no assessment will be made of the extent to which the Great Powers should maintain the United Nations Organization as the 'sole guardian of world peace in the future'. Nor will it be suggested, as one visiting American sociologist has, that a great reorganization is needed in British society if Britain is to maintain the standard of living to which she has been accustomed in the past. An account will be given instead of the nature of political action—an account whose purpose will be to explain, not what the author would wish political action were like now and not what he supposes to be a constituent of successful action in the future, but what he takes political men to be doing in advanced (or complicated) societies; and whose usefulness can be tested by its success in making intelligible the various subject-matters which yield material for the study of political practice.

The distinguishing characteristics of political action are the tendency of those who engage in it to consider the circumstances in which it is to be taken (and the limitations this imposes on the freedom of their choice), the uncertainty of the consequences it is likely to produce (with the consequent difficulty in being sure that action is right): and the arbitrariness of the assumptions within which it is conducted which arises from the fact that it is not normally politicians alone who create the social and intellectual climate or power situation in which they work, but everyone else who exercises influence in the society of which they are a part. Above all, it is characterized by the fact that, in spite of the reticence, deception and arbitrariness in which it is involved, in spite of the limitation of its effectiveness and the uncertainty of its consequences, it is, notwithstanding, the outcome of a form of practical reasoning, which is not less autonomous because its limits are close, which is not less valid because it is concerned with a best than can be done in circumstances that exist, rather than a best possible in circumstances that do not; and which can be judged in the first place according to its own conventions by those who are engaged in it and, ultimately, like any other activity, by the judgement, whatever that is taken to mean, of God.

All political action displays these characteristics, not just action which is taken as it was intended and not just when intentions are announced in advance of action. All political action is an attempt to take account of the circumstances: and even if the circumstances of which the actor takes account turn out to be irrelevant to the objective at which he was aiming, this is still what he is trying to do. Even if the circumstances surrounding a decision about a question of public policy are less important than the circumstances that will affect his reputation, circumstances will still be what a politician is trying to consider: and this will be true even when his understanding of the nature of the circumstances is defective. Imperfect understanding may involve failure or it may not: it may produce sensible policies or again it may not: it may damage society, or may advance its health: but, whatever the consequences, history will not show any politician of importance who is not *trying* to understand: and if it does, the history will have been based on a misconception. Statesmen do not in practice ask what an ideal intimation would indicate in an ideal situation: they decide in the particular situation with which they are confronted whatever they feel it possible to decide: and if they do not, someone else will exercise the power they supposed was theirs. Political action is not a romantic symphony of purpose and ideal, but a matter of specific decision and specific calculation designed to produce ends which, however uncertain, are limited. Even when ignorance means that decisions are taken in the dark, this is so: and it is so even when a politician does not know what to expect of the consequences of an action for which he is responsible. Just as a foreign secretary may, in an immobile and unfavourable diplomatic situation, toss a pebble into the pond with no more exact feeling than that the situation could not possibly be made worse by being made different, so an opposition party, in face of an overwhelming majority, may feel that any action—even the action of provoking a public split amongst its leaders—might be better than action taken out of exact calculation. In both cases there is uncertainty and something approaching irresponsibility: but in both, nevertheless, there is not only specific choice, but also a specific objective—to improve the diplomatic standing of the Power, or the political standing of the party, concerned. Even the great revolutionary moments, when all the barriers seem to be down and all limitations removed, are probably not, when viewed from the standpoint of the actors, like that at all. The rapidity of events may reduce the area of regularity and the time available for decision, and may greatly increase uncertainty about the outcome: but, even where language of spectacular generality is used in order to recommend orders to those who are expected to obey them, the orders will be as specific and exact as those who give them judge it necessary to make them.

No doubt power can be gained by men who make no effort to take account of the circumstances in which they act: and no doubt politicians who disregard the circumstances can achieve a measure of success. Luck, chance or accident, however, are unlikely indefinitely to save an unregarding politician from the consequences of his nature. Politicians need both to do what they think ought to be done and to have whatever power they think necessary to doing it. There is no necessary correlation between governing well and remaining in office: and the 'relevant circumstances' include not only the general circumstances of the society in which government is conducted but the political and personal circumstances which give a politician the opportunity to conduct it. Political power is amongst men contested, and even though luck may for a time delay the reckoning, there is no reason why it should for ever armour a politician against failure to be relevant to the circumstances in which he has to act.

It was objected, at an earlier stage in this book, that the claim that 'the State must control society' was a persuasive, not an explanatory, statement. Even as a persuasion to action, however, it is absurd. It may be that there are moments in the history of any society when the political power becomes so great that those who control it have the very widest range of choice possible. In societies also where economic development is retarded, political power may sometimes be unusually concentrated and unusually powerful (though even a 'despot' who faces no 'feudal' resistance cannot entirely ignore the opinions of his subjects). But in highly developed and complicated communities, unpolitical forces almost invariably impose restriction on the political. Hitler in 1936, Sir Winston Churchill's Government in 1941 and Stalin after 1928, probably had greater freedom to do exactly as they wanted in 'controlling society' than other governments have ever had in anything resembling modern societies. Yet in 1945 Hitler was dead and his work in ruins: and Sir Winston Churchill's Government was dissolved. Stalin, it is true, remained: but it is doubtful whether the Russia which emerged from the war of 1941 was the Russia Stalin had intended to create in 1928. Sometimes those who control the machinery of government can edge society along the path they think it ought to follow: sometimes they cannot. In some communities the State is more powerful than in others and there are variations in the extent to which it is the instrument, or creator, of a dominant social class. In some societies political power is one way to wealth and social standing: and if this is not so in contemporary England, it was in some parts of the seventeenth and eighteenth centuries and is so in some other societies now.

In some communities the State is so powerful, and its purposes so revolutionary, that political concerns impregnate every area of human activity. But even when impregnation is greatest, even when the political authority probes, directs, restricts and persecutes most extensively, the degree of control it exercises is limited by the fact that the passage of the generations and the deviousness of its subjects' reactions are too vast to be controlled by even the most determined use of governmental machinery. To kill criticism by killing critics (as Hitler and Stalin did) increases the area of control. Modern communications and modern weapons make control still easier. But weapons and communications are manned by men who are capable of choice. They have their opinions (even if not normally articulate about them): and when ambition, misunderstanding or anger drive them to distrust their rulers, they will move. In totalitarian régimes, the difficulty of changing, or restricting the power of, government is great: the penalty for failure drastic. But the fact that influential opinions are held by those who control the machinery of suppression, instead of by free voters and members of parliament, does not alter the fact that the Soviet Government, like any other government, is poised at a point of calculated balance between the conflicting ambitions which keep its political structure in equilibrium. The more closely the politics of any society is examined, the clearer it will become that, in using the doctrines and following the purposes to which their elders wish them to be committed, each generation and (within each generation) the various groups show an inventiveness and originality which cannot be destroyed. Inventiveness need not be self-conscious: nor does it necessarily involve deliberate public posturing. The literary vapourings by which the literary intelligentsia sometimes judges the passage of the generations are in no way essential to political change. In the Soviet Union, as everywhere else, those who produce and distribute goods, those who control the machinery of government, those who teach and those who work at every social level are, whether they know it or not, making, daily, innumerable political, social and economic choices, of which some will respond to the wishes of the political Power and of which some will not: but the general direction of which must, because it is cumulative, not only be outside the control of government but outside its range of vision also. Statesmen may, as the years pass, continue to make the assumptions about their subjects' wishes that seemed relevant when they first came to power. They may comfort themselves with the illusion that they do in fact know where society is going. Of the changes which the mere passage of time causes they may know little: and so long as these changes are uncoordinated, this will not matter much. But each element of change, small in itself and unselfconsciously accomplished, grows, by addition, into significance. Each alteration, obscure by itself at the hands of no one of particular importance, becomes, in conjunction with everything else, of the greatest importance possible. And suddenly a statesman or régime awakens to the fact that its views no longer command assent, that its words no longer command attention and that the slogans uttered or intentions announced ten years before seem, even to those who grew up beneath their shadow, irrelevant and insubstantial nonsense.

No régime has total control over the society it governs and it is necessary, in considering the development of any particular society, to understand, not just the actions and intentions of those who govern, but the efforts of all men whatever their status or occupation. At any particular moment those who exercise social influence

183

exercise it, not just according to the requirements of the political power, but according to the responsibility they feel to do the right thing—which may or may not be right but which is the only safeguard and security society has that its affairs will be conducted to advantage. Nevertheless, if political power is not, for all the dignity with which its exponents continue to surround it, as great as is sometimes claimed, it is not for that reason less real. A political group may, by being in the right place at the right time, edge events, not *exactly* as it would like them to go, but in what it thinks the right direction. Within limits imposed by the power of unpolitical people, political action has a measure of autonomy and political persons, between themselves, something resembling professional conventions. Amongst those who exercise power there is no doubt the same combination of calculation and thoughtlessness, scheming and simplicity, competence and blundering, avarice, ambition and altruism, stupidity, sense and sanctimoniousness as there is amongst all other men in all other of their dealings with one another. The prizes open to those who are ambitious in this area of activity appeal to a certain sort of imagination: but they are not more desirable (to those who want them) than the others that are found in universities and boardrooms, messes and laboratories and all other of the normal areas in which energy can find an outlet. Those who rule do not need to operate openly in order to act sensibly: nor do they need to give reasons in order to act rationally. They have, from education and experience, habit, discipline and choice, 'reasonable' ways of exercising whatever power they have. And in a significant sense they are, and must be, irresponsible. They work within conventional and legal limits. There are things they know they cannot do and things they know they cannot say.

There are slogans that must be uttered and slogans that must in no circumstances be uttered at all: but, so long as some of the conventions are observed, there is very little they cannot get away with. There are degrees of responsibility: but the competence of those who exercise power in any particular society can in the nature of the case be judged by themselves and their equals, and by hardly anyone else.

Those who approach the highest reaches of political power are, unlikely, at any rate in public, to use words as very much more than tools for the accomplishment of their purposes and unlikely to expect from the words they use relevance except to the object in view. Words uttered in public by statesmen in the conduct of political practice are designed, not as philosophical words ought to be, to be aids to understanding, but to have consequences in the world of practice. Not all words used by statesmen are of this sort. Statesmen, like others, feel on occasion compelled to tell the truth or unloose their anger whatever the damage. In practice, also, between equals and where no question of public statement is involved, statesmen no doubt say what they think, conduct themselves in a manner relevant to their situations and speak openly or discreetly according to character, background and judgement of suitability. Words, further, take hold of those who use them. Words constantly repeated, slogans repeatedly reiterated, incline men who begin by believing in nothing but their persuasive utility to put into practice the policies they enjoin. Nothing is more common in public discussion in this country than the young politician, anxious to show himself progressive and intelligent (particularly when he is rich, or Conservative), uttering the platitudes about governmental action which liberal opinion has thrust upon him. All, no doubt, he intends is to use words to establish an image in the public eye: to prove to high (but progressive) intellects in Cross Street or Printing House Square that even rich men can talk the language of Mill. But whatever he intends, slogans of this sort used in the first place in a cynical manner to acclimatize a party to the tone of the prevailing intelligentsia, strike roots so deep in the minds of even the most conservative of politicians that only the passage of the generations—if even that—can remove them.

Nevertheless, whatever the intended consequences of words, statesmen and politicians (when using words used also in philosophical discourse) are not using them in the same way or with the same object as a philosopher. Nor do they necessarily wish to contribute to serious discussion of public issues. Robespierre, proclaiming that all men are equal, was not using the word *equality* in the same way or with the same object as an explanatory political philosopher. Nor, we may take it, did Sir David Ormsby-Gore have the same intention as Mr Gunnar Myrdal would have had if it had been Mr Myrdal (and not the British ambassador-designate to Washington) who had observed that the late Mr Hammarskjold 'appealed always to reason and to the facts' and was 'possessed by a deep conviction that through the United Nations a better world could be built, a world free from war and free from want'.[1] Bismarck's *Recollections* (and his speeches) no more tell the truth about Bismarck's life than foreign secretaries will about Suez or Catherine de Medici about the massacre of Saint Bartholomew. Rightly or wrongly the stability of all political societies is thought to depend on a certain measure of calculated deception. Most régimes wish to present to their public and posterity greater rectitude than they think they have: and it is necessary to judge the utterances of govern-

[1] *The Listener*, 21 September 1961, p. 417.

ments in the light of the possibility that the obvious official material is riddled with significant reticences.

'Political decisions' vary in scale from beginning a war to modifying a word in a telegram. No doubt, in taking decisions of the first magnitude statesmen follow their judgement of the interests of society at large according to the duties they conceive themselves committed to undertake. Even here, individual calculation or individual anger may be of importance. In general, however, on the largest issues, the magnitude of the consequences would probably impose on even the most cynical politician a measure of self-denial. At any other level, on the other hand, there is reason to expect every sort of personal calculation to affect judgement. Nor is there any reason either to regret that this is so, or to suggest that action taken out of this sort of irrelevance is necessarily bad. Irrelevance, inadvertence and ambition are the sustaining material of political activity. There is little reason to imagine that action taken out of what appears at the time to be 'relevant' motive is alone likely to be suitable, and even less to imagine that a means of making political decisions from which personal ambition and political calculation had been removed, would, if feasible, be more certainly effective than any other. That is no reason why it should not be attempted, if anyone thinks it worth the effort of trying to do so. But those who desire to see it work should not necessarily suppose that it is likely to improve the quality of government as a consequence.

This is not to say that political action is normally taken, as it were, out of intuition or chance alone. Some actions are certainly taken out of random irrelevancy when a person is mad or has not geared himself to the subject under consideration. There is no reason to suppose that this sort of action can never have reasonable consequences, though it is reasonable to assume that it will not do so often. Most political actions are taken as a result of deliberate purposes being premeditated, deliberated choices made and deliberate account taken of the circumstances in which decisions become necessary: and if this were a world which responded fully to this sort of deliberation, that would be sufficient to ensure success. Unfortunately, however, it is not. Many things which happen as a result of what seems to the actor to be choice happen, when looked at from another level, as a result of chance. And in explanation of specific historical events, it is not always easy to know which level to choose. As soon as a political choice has been made, self-respect involves politicians in pretending that they intended the consequences. Nor is it easy to be sure whether a politician who makes claims for the consequences of his intentions, either intended the consequences to happen, conceived the possibility that they might, or thought it sensible that they should.

Nor conversely, when a politician is seen saying that he will perform some large political act and is then seen performing it, is it necessarily right to say that he predicted it. In all these questions circumstances are important. What a politician, taking account of the circumstances, says about what he will do is one thing: what he does in circumstances different from those he predicted is another. Political action cannot be understood in isolation from its surroundings: and the character and consequences of an act cannot be understood without seeing them in the setting in which they occur. If a Chancellor of the Exchequer promises in October to reduce income tax in the April following and if, then, he does reduce income tax in April, then he may seem to have been doing what he predicted. But if, between October and April, there is a trade recession, a balance of payments crisis and rising domestic demand, then the act of reducing income tax (though in itself the act he predicted) is not in any other important sense the act he said he would perform—because, in the different circumstances, it has a different significance and because different consequences are likely to follow. Indeed, the more closely one looks at the largest political actions, the more difficult it is to be certain that statesmen do in fact predict what they are going to do. Neither statesmen nor governments have comprehensive views of the probable consequences of any particular action: and this seriously restricts their ability to predict.

The limitations we have been describing operate in all societies and there is no need, in these respects, to make much of the differences between the differing forms of government. The difference between the method of accumulating political support in a parliamentary democracy and the method by which it is accumulated in any other society is that, whereas, in the one, power is accumulated as much by organizing opinion as by organizing interests, in the other opinions need much more usually to be supported by the instruments of coercion before they can become effective. The characteristic defects of each arrangement—the tendency in one case for opinion to become effective without regard to interest and the tendency in the other for coercion to be used indiscriminately and destructively—are considerable, and it should never be supposed that the defects of a parliamentary régime are necessarily greater than the different defects of the alternatives. A major function of Parliament in Britain is to provide seventy or eighty men who can control the machinery of government. It is not necessary to suppose that seventy or eighty men could not emerge in some other way—by marriage, descent, or competitive examination, by intrigue in palaces and corridors (as, indeed, to some extent they do now) or by recurrent military revolution. If existing arrangements do in fact survive, it will not be because they represent eternal principles or because they are 'democratic', 'rational' or unusually 'right' but because they are parts of the furniture of English life which have been insufficiently objectionable to be destroyed and because skill, premeditation and luck will have been dedicated to preserving them. It is difficult for scholars who attempt to give an account of any particular society not to see in it a reflection of their own preoccupations and more difficult still for intelligent, cultivated, articulate, writers who are committed to a belief in the value of Parliamentary democracy to understand that the particular activity in which they are interested may not be as important as they would like to think. To speak of 'Britain' as a 'parliamentary democracy', by concentrating attention on the public part of the *political* process by which governments are chosen, suggests that this is the most important characteristic of British political arrangements. From paying attention to the behaviour of Parliament, of ministers in Parliament and of parties and the public during elections, it tends to be suggested that the safety or health of society is the preoccupation only of those who exercise specifically political power. From studying the language of public political discussion, it tends to be assumed, not that governments are invariably disingenuous in public, but that they ought not to be. And when the public appearance of power is thought to be different from the private one, it tends to be implied that Parliament must be given more power, that insurance companies and industrial corporations must be subjected to public control or that it should be made more difficult for any decision to be taken by anyone without extensive public discussion. The caucuses which in both

190

parties select parliamentary candidates (and in many constituencies effectively choose M.P.'s) are supposed to constitute an affront to the representative principle: whereas the explanatory conclusion to which consideration of their processes might usefully lead is not that existing arrangements are falling back in their struggle to be (in this very limited sense) representative, but that the conventions by which M.P.'s emerge in this country are not usefully described by this word. In all these cases the public slogan provides a misleading explanation of the reality. Some men have office and others want it: some men are politicians from duty or hereditary opportunity, others from ambition, idleness or accident; and even if those who have office or power believe themselves to be operating a representative system, ambition is normally geared to fulfilling specific duties, advancing particular causes or gaining personal objectives rather than to maintaining anything so general as a 'representative system'. If office is to be gained, power exercised or duty done, it is necessary to press, or persuade, those who exercise political influence to adopt particular courses of action, but there is no reason to suppose that *public* pressure is the most successful way of doing it. Men are promoted and causes advanced not so that scholars may judge the outcome, but so that those who have power may exercise it according to their own standard of fitness and convenience. Public discussion and public reasons are by no means the most important, and no confidence, or doubt, need be felt about the wisdom of a political decision because the newspapers or 'responsible opinion' have, or have not, discussed it.

Societies can be governed as effectively with little public discussion as with much. Parliament does not need to do its business in public in order to be useful: and there is no reason to think that the health of society in general owes more to the efficiency of Parliament than to the energy and activity of those who exercise power elsewhere. At least as important as the appearance of public political discussion is the existence of what may be thought a powerful ruling-class which may from time to time err and which may, indeed, be corrupted by the slogans it has come to use but which is not less tough, powerful or authoritative because it works through Parliament and an elective system. Even if it provides no permanent safeguard, manipulation of the opinions of electors is a safeguard against revolutionary change which has, together with political and economic luck, been effective in the last decade in cushioning the shock of radical assault on the existing social structure.

Some political scientists recognize that this is so. Advertising in particular has presented a problem to those who believe that the principles implicit in British political arrangements require that no party should have 'an enormous advantage in the political battle'. Since a connection is assumed between society's health, open discussion, parliamentary decision and their own social usefulness, an arbitrary standard of parliamentary control and public decision is assumed and it is implied that a society in which these features are not as prominent as they would be in an 'ideal' English society cannot be a good society at all. There may be (there often is), amongst those who exercise great influence, conflict between one interest and another: and the academic interest among others is one. Dons who make their reputations by writing and speaking may attach importance to the existence of political checks (through public discussion) on the power of stockbrokers, and Civil Servants, company directors and the large corporations. Dons may, like others, voice the dissatisfactions felt by citizens at the actions of all the agencies which make an impact on their lives. But if they are not in practice to be blamed for this, they ought still in explanation to recognize that stockbrokers, Civil Servants, company directors and the large corporations contribute as much to the 'rationality' of society as they do: and that no greater importance, significance or rationality should necessarily be imputed to their own actions than to the actions of these others.

If it be objected that this suggests that it can be 'rational' for a few men to exercise a political and economic power and political and intellectual influence very much greater than the influence exercised by others, it must be answered that the recurrent existence of such disproportion is one of the plainest facts of human history. In every generation some men have had more power than others just as some also have had more wealth, more talent and greater ambition: and, without the use which these few men make of their skill, intelligence and organizing sense, the majority of mankind could expect neither the benefits that accompany civilization on the one hand, nor the danger which conflict amongst their leaders entails on the other.

Not all the consequences of this dependence are agreeable. Some may sometimes be avoided by deliberately limiting the power these few men exercise: but even if limits are imposed (as Professor Titmuss, for example, wants them imposed in Britain) on the power of industrial firms and insurance companies to make decisions which affect large numbers of citizens without reference to the citizens concerned, this might merely transfer some part of this power from one group of men (accountants perhaps) to the hands of others (members of parliament, ministers, Civil Servants and the sort of don who sits on Royal Commissions). The uselessness of explanatory dogmatism is nowhere better illustrated than by consideration of suggestions of this sort. Is it more likely to produce a 'rational', 'responsible', or 'free' society if the wielders of industrial power are left as free from political interference as they would like? Will they pay more attention to public pressure if public pressure is brought to bear through newspapers and trade unions instead of through Parliament or the Civil Service? Are parliamentary control and the political power so weak in England that their influence needs to be increased? or are they stronger in all directions than they have ever been before? Once the platitudes of the higher journalism are examined in this way, it becomes clear that they ask questions to which answers cannot be given. It is impossible to estimate the consequences of changes of this sort. It is not just the political power and not just the deliberate purposes of the political authority which will determine the character of society in the future, but every act performed by anyone who exercises influence—whether in controlling an industry or making a decision in a government department: and any attempt to pretend that the *political* interest has a monopoly of rationality is mistaken.

It is, of course, likely that statesmen who use persuasive words long enough and successfully enough will come to be influenced by them as well. It may also be that the capacity to manipulate opinion, command assent and accumulate support by public parade of prejudice or public display of conscience may be a poor preparation for leading a Cabinet or controlling a department of State. It is possible that this sort of success produces an eccentric or inadequate style of ruler. Nevertheless, words have such great potential consequences that they tend to be treated with a pragmatic practicality appropriate to dealing with any sort of power. And since words have consequences, consequences must be taken into account, and intentions weighed in the scale of moral judgement not only according to the intentions which are enunciated but also according to the consequences that ensue. It is not sufficient to imagine that truths of practice have been proclaimed if the truths turn out to be impracticable: even though resolution in pragmatic, historical terms of the question—which morality is going to prevail?—provides no answer to the question, which is right? The one that does prevail may well be evil and its utility in the experience of mankind may be to remind us that it is. Once a man has reached a certain stage of autonomy, he will act rightly or wrongly, morally or immorally, according to his success in using the activities in which he is engaged for the ends they have come to fulfil. In all activities, worth resides in the competence with which the activity is accomplished as well as the end to which it is turned; and not just in the fluency with which ends are announced in advance of action. There is a hard lesson to be learnt by those who are fluent but have no power—that while it may just possibly be true that power tends to corrupt, nothing corrupts more absolutely than the certainty that power will never be given to a man to subject his opinions to the unpredictable test of responsible action.

Deeply embedded in most political action and all political structures, and unavoidable in all political calculation, are entrenched interests which do not yield to the mere expression of moral preference, and it is common for each person, group, corporation or nation to pursue its interests without particular regard for the interests of others. This, however, does not mean that moral consideration is irrelevant to political action or that attempts to act in a way which a person conceives to be right are irrelevant. At the same time as the limited radical self-righteousness is rejected, the radical confidence in men's ability to predict and control the consequences of their actions should be rejected also. Because the consequences of most large-scale political action are in general unpredictable, we conclude, not that no action should ever be taken or only action to further what are conceived to be interests, but that, since both action and inaction taken with a view to interests may well have results different from those that are anticipated, very little can be said for asserting the necessary value of one sort of action—an interested action (or a disinterested one for that matter)—in defiance of other preferences arising from different sources; and none whatever for supposing that intimation of suitability can be known to be right more certainly in one case than in another. In short, since whatever action is taken, the consequences are likely in general to be unpredictable, governments (as well as persons) might as well do what they think right or appropriate in the circumstances, and may well allow themselves to be moved by whatever combination of convenience and prejudice they find to hand, even if that does not immediately advance their interests. Also, it may not be wrong (though it is not necessarily right) to be directed by a prudence which will prevent unlimited moral preoccupation overriding all other concerns and to try always to maintain practical intentions beneath the shadow of the thought that, since the moral self-righteousness by which they are generated may well have effects less important than chance, or the accidental movements of events, dignity would be gained if those who maintain them moderated their zeal and put a curb on their enthusiasm. This may seem a slender justification for the attempt to exercise moral influence in political action and a fragile basis for the operation of higher political purposes: and so it is and that is what it is intended to be. All political institutions rest on bases which are only moderately susceptible to control by each generation. They are rendered only marginally firmer by their considerable antiquity and the fact that policy is subjected to discussion: and those who claim explanatory or philosophical authority in passing judgement on governments which do not meet their moral requirements should bear in mind the fact that this is so.

It is necessary to insist still further on the arbitrariness of the course of political activity, on the transient character of the benefits that flow from it and on the damage done to attempts at understanding which flow from the belief that political action can provide something more. The conventional liberties enjoyed in this and other 'democratic' States do not owe their validity to the tendency of democratic thinkers to justify them by reference to doctrines of equality, social contract and natural right. They arise, on the contrary, from accidental circumstances, the by-product of conflict between groups, classes, interests, intentions and religions, when conflict has reached deadlock and produced practical equilibrium: and they are to be respected not because these freedoms are necessarily desirable in themselves, but because they are part of the accepted furniture of British politics. This may be thought an uncertain basis on which to maintain a free press, keep innocent citizens out of prison or Parliament open, and it must be admitted that it is. This, however, is not surprising. The conventional freedoms are not enjoyed in every society in the world and have not been enjoyed in an absolutely untempered way in this. And it is possible, to say the least, that they will continue to flourish only so long as those who use them most do not allow them to damage the bases of the political structure.

No doubt there is a tendency—once these freedoms

have been established—to produce reasons to justify their existence. No doubt it makes for stability that the reasons should be believed while the benefits are enjoyed. But there is a gap between this sort of consecrating reflection and explanation of the course of events from which they emerged. A political structure, once it has come into existence through the arbitrary exercise of power and an arbitrary conjunction of circumstances, tends to accumulate around itself a covering of conventional habits, reasonable laws, acceptable customs and well-understood liberties which are then taken to have a validity of their own. Around these conventional structures fantasies of principle are woven: and from the existence of any particular set of conventions, it tends to be argued that the conventions themselves are necessary marks of good government. A rigidity develops in speaking of the political structure—as though the fantasies produced to justify the original act were essential to all settled societies; and exaggerations—about liberty, about rights and about the content of the conscience of civilized men—deflect philosophers from understanding not only the arbitrariness of the original act but also the fact that, without the original arbitrary exercise of power and a recurring willingness (where necessary) to repeat it, the political structure could not exist at all. Slogans, prejudices (even the prejudice of appealing for rational consideration) which profess to appeal to truths necessary to society, demonstrate only the extent to which the energies of political men and the conventions of political society are dominated by the (philosophically misconceived) attempt to see the arbitrary course of events as the simple embodiment of principle. But if this is so, it must in explanation be accepted that the chief function of the public expression of political opinions is to generate support for men, parties or groups so that there may, in the volatile circumstances in which all societies exist, always be alternative governments which command political capital sufficient to do whatever a government may have to do. Most of these opinions have the appearance of slogans and it is difficult to see how they could be anything else. To imagine that the detailed opinions of politicians without power, or journalists without office, have specific practical relevance, or need more precise definition than will accumulate assent or express discontent in the crudest and most intelligible way, is to be guilty of a faith in the efficacy of opinion worthy almost of Mill himself.

It is not surprising that the tendency to use words in this way draws a veil over the workings of government. Since political decision yields sparingly to premeditated principle, slogans useful to accumulating support may be irrelevant to a departmental minute. Sometimes concealment is made in order to maintain reputations: and 'sometimes' to say openly what has been done is safer than politicians suppose. Often, however, if the truth were told, their followers would not understand: the political climate would demand condemnation of what they knew to be necessary and no smaller stock of political virtue should be imputed to those who conceal than to those who tell the truth. Nor need concealment of this sort be subjected to condemnation in advance of action. Judgement of the point at which reticence will do more damage than frankness, or frankness than reticence, is a matter of responsibility for individuals who have power: and if that seems a fragile basis for maintaining the political equilibrium, it is no more fragile than society has ever had and no more deplorable. The extent of the responsibility devolving on individual politicians in matters of this sort is lightened by the establishment of rules, the maintenance of customary procedures, and the operation of governmental conventions which can be observed by those who operate them without strain or difficulty. The irrelevant philosophic mind, anxious to impose its concern for truth on all activities, will no doubt think it regrettable that deception should be practised in public political discussion. But those who have responsibility to govern may not be wrong in thinking it better that citizens should be deceived and peaceful where they might have been bursting with truth and burning with resentment.

Scepticism about the relation between a politician's public intentions and his private actions should not suggest that it is wrong for a politician to have conscious political purposes. Between the enunciation of political purposes and their accomplishment in practice, however, there is a complicated process to be passed through before any of them acquire practical significance. It is never reasonable to assert that, if a different succession of choices had been taken, more desirable consequences would have ensued. Still less is it sensible to argue that, if greater consistency had been displayed in following general, pre-articulated doctrines, the movement of history would have been disciplined more effectively than it has been. Although it is open to men, groups, classes or nations to be moved by limited, precise plans or large doctrinal purposes (if either helps to accumulate support), it is idle to expect the ceaseless movement of events to be predictably responsive to the wishes even of those who control much power and might be expected to have a greater chance of giving practical effect to their wishes. Whatever the merits of the doctrine a man enunciates, however impeccable the preparation he makes (before he has power), to whatever lengths his attention to the traditions of his society carry him in avoiding the temptations which events and his own ambition thrust upon him, it is always possible that his intentions will be thwarted by events, it is always likely that he will have to traffic with error, and his most dogmatically misguided opponents may always accidentally act rightly, and his most zealous supporters wrongly, in the indeterminate world of political action.

It is necessary, then, if governments are to be obeyed, that they should command respect. It is essential, if régimes are to be free of the uncertainty which comes from having always to underpin authority, that the people should have confidence in them. Confidence comes at least as much from the appearance they give as from anything they do in office. Nevertheless, however desirable it may be that statesmen should *seem* to be men of principle and however important it is that subjects should have confidence in their rectitude, there lies beneath the public parade of principle at which all governments and most statesmen make an effort, every sort of uncertainty which loyalty cannot deal with and every sort of circumstance which principle is incapable of commanding. That loyalty is necessary cannot be disputed: that 'principle', as much as 'interest', is the material of public loyalty in democratic communities cannot be denied. But this does not alter the fact that, behind the great edifices reared by public discussion, behind the admiration felt for Roosevelt or Churchill or de Gaulle, there is, as well as stern resolute government and the effort at pursuing the practical implications of the principles to which statesmen are committed, every sort of inadequacy and incompetence besides. The desire to see 'men of principle' conducting the most important affairs with which the political community can entrust them is a matter of consequence to the body politic as a whole. The extent of a politician's control over events, however, is small, his range of influence narrow. Confidence arises from what people think a régime is like, not necessarily from what it *is* like: and it is not only cynicism which suggests that the most useful sort of politician in a 'democratic' community may well be the man of principle who has a set of principles to suit *every* situation.

IV

IN A WORLD, therefore, where neither mere power nor
mere articulateness provides any assurance of goodness
or rationality, where no correlation exists between the
two but where the possession of either gives great opportunities for achieving both, prejudice commits a man to
many important positions: and whoever has the most
authoritative prejudices is, as it were, sovereign. Authority here is of the greatest significance. Government may
be defined as those who happen to have political authority in the society in which they live, and the ruling-class
as those who happen to have all sorts of other authority
as well. They are not for that reason more virtuous or
sensible than anyone else (though they are not necessarily less sensible or less rational either). Every political
and social structure is an arbitrary thing—where society
happens to have got to at the time. The authority of
law, the authority of fact and the authority of power in
this sense are the same thing and any pretence that they
are not involves a flight from a limiting and disagreeable
reality. They are in fact all men have—power geared to
support the opinions, interests, preferences and desires of
those who happen for reasons as various as the situations
themselves to command authority at any particular time.
Nor does the fact that opinions, interests, preferences and
desires are to some extent imposed, make it any more
difficult for society to act sensibly or rationally in the
future. All human activity depends on recurrent exclu-
sion of certain lines of advance—exploration of the
decision that some assumptions are sterile, meaningless

or unhelpful. Since most opinions, when worked on for long periods by high and sustained intelligence, can be moulded into regular, rational shape, there seems to be no reason why these facts should be disagreeable. And which assumptions are held may often matter very much less than the explanatory use to which they are put.

This may seem illiberal but that does not make it any the less true that it applies to all human activity. It describes not just the discipline imposed by the Communist party or the Roman Church but the discipline supported by the laws and conventions of liberal States also. And it applies to the means by which all traditions of intellectual explanation are maintained. All traditions of thinking and all traditions of action involve constant rejection of what is taken to be unhelpful and the impulse to press to the limit of possibility assumptions which have, arbitrarily no doubt, been accepted as useful. Liberty here is very closely limited. Scientists who use their freedom to adopt views about their own professional interests fundamentally at variance with the views of those who exercise professional authority over them are no more likely to have access to the expensive equipment necessary to scientific experiment than are theologians who profess perverse opinions to occupy influential pulpits or dons who maintain odd professional assumptions to occupy posts of professional importance. Curtailment of liberty involved in judgement of this sort constitutes what is normally thought of as the legitimate exercise of professional authority. Curtailments of liberty are thought intolerable only when those who have no professional authority, and no experience of the matters with which they deal, insist on making decisions about them. Even here distinctions have to be drawn. No one would think it sensible, in existing conditions, for a government department to define the scientific relevance of a scientific theory or to decide whether Cromwell's followers after 1649 were part of a declining gentry or a rising one. English governments have in the past, however, made what look like definitions of the truth of theological propositions and it is difficult to see how they could have avoided doing so. Even academic explanation has consequences in political practice, and if the consequences are great and immediate, it is difficult to say categorically that governments must avoid responsibility. When scientific claims to absolute freedom conflict with the duty the political authority has to perform its own functions in what it takes to be its own sphere, it is not easy to say which is right. A scientist working for a government department does not suppose that he will avoid punishment if he reveals his own discoveries to the State's enemies, and the government of almost any State would think it necessary to prevent him revealing some sorts of important discovery even if he were not. Complaints from scientists who have been prevented from conducting experiments dangerous to public health would not always be thought unanswerable. In all these matters liberty to speak, print and express opinions, and liberty to put opinions into practice, are restricted in the activity itself by those who exercise professional authority, and in the wider political area by the authority exercised by the wielders of the public power. Between authority drawn from one activity and authority drawn from another there is often considerable conflict, which can be resolved in fact only by the success the political interest supporting each has in making its claim effective. But whatever detailed alteration is produced by conflict itself, society's course continues successfully or unsuccessfully, sensibly or foolishly, as energy is turned into directions judged useful by those who set the pace in any of the activities in which men engage, and displays in the full accomplishment of practice the fruitfulness or sterility of the assumptions from which they start and the prejudices by which they are directed.

Men are, then, over very large areas, in the grip of, dependent on, and in one sense determined by, conditions over which they have no means of exercising conscious control. They are not responsible for the families into which they were born, the education they are given or the station in which they live: and they are less responsible than they sometimes like to pretend for the experience they accumulate, the temperaments they suffer, the ambitions by which they are moved and the choices they make. It may even be that a man is in temperament what he is always likely to be at fifteen or sixteen and will not change significantly thereafter. Men are, in this sense, not responsible for the constituent ingredients of their character, though they are for the measure in which the ingredients are mixed and the outcome of the mixture. And explanation is inadequate totally to explain the movement of events on which men move or fully to grasp the relationship between a man and his environment. All human activity in principle is open to comprehension by those who assume that a measure of rationality is implicit in it. But the practical limitations the human intelligence finds in making intelligible the world around it are considerable. And, just as in all other explanatory activity there can be no finality but only the constant effort to show what is the case, so, in political activity, there is a constant effort also to do what is right. Political activity, like all other activity, is an attempt to make the ceaseless flow of the world yield a moral content and moral consequences by subjecting it to a moral and rational will of whose proper direction we are not altogether certain. There can be no certainty that any particular action is right. Even when the nature of the circumstances and the limitations it imposes are grasped, the difficulties in the way of judging action right or wrong are considerable: and no judgement at any particular moment can be more than temporary and tentative. Without knowledge of the nature of the activity in which the will is operating, there can be nothing resembling judgement at all: but if right action can be taken—by accident as it were, because the consequences are good—this does not make the difficulty of impartial judgement or rational appreciation any the less great. In practice each man will believe what he is doing to be for the best: but in explanation the philosopher can only confess his ignorance of the place an action will take in the history of the world.

Action in order to be right or rational need not necessarily be self-conscious. Every man has a limited amount of energy to hand and diversion of energy from the task of acting (according to practical judgement in the circumstances) to the task of reflecting in advance about the rightness of actions, can in a practical sense be energy wasted. Principles without practical content are rhetoric. Practical content is added only when principles are geared to a subject-matter and the principles and the subject-matter welded together in unselfconscious unity, not by preaching or reflection or exhortation on every occasion in advance of action but by the outcome of ingrained habit, habitual reaction, unproblematical judgement which flows from the response of a mind adequately soaked in the difficulties of its situation.

The point of practical contact, therefore, between principle, intention and ideal on the one hand and political practice on the other occurs, not just at the trivial conscientious crises when men flaunt their principles or consult their consciences in self-conscious panic, but in the broad certainty of spontaneous response which adequate habit provides. It is the whole of the education and the whole of a religion that a man has, not just his reflective philosophy, which determines what part he sees of the world and what he will think it necessary to do in it. In this sense the only practical guarantee that men will act in a way thought suitable by those around them arises from the attitudes inculcated through the education they have had—from family and friends as well as from schools and teachers: and this continuity of behaviour is the only serious guarantee that persons and nations will act rightly in the maintenance of sensible political conventions. Even here it is impossible to predict the outcome of the education or religion a child may have. But so far as men have any guarantee for the future, this is where it can be most effective. In this process no one source is likely to be dominant and even the family will have only a limited effect (and not necessarily the one intended by the parent). Education, however, means education, not indoctrination: the gradual acquisition of the capacity to do something, not the mere infusion of opinions. In a narrow political sense, it means seeing at close quarters how politicians act (rather than knowing what journalists or political philosophers do to explain it, or how historians have accounted for the pieces of it they know about from the past), and, in the broadest sense, in having adequate relationships with the other members of the society in which one lives. Reflective explanation has an influence (and in sharpening the mind considerable utility): but it is only a small part of the whole. In preparing men to respond to the situations by which they are confronted, political philosophers have a responsibility. But the responsibility is shared with all citizens in every example they give to all others and is not the concern of political philosophers alone. The object of the study to which we invite attention, then, begins from the point at which the gap between mind and the world it inhabits becomes manifest. It is not the only problem which stimulates the philosopher or historian and it does not contain the whole task of either. But adequate historical writing revealing Mind wrestling with circumstance, and coherent metaphysics, explaining that these difficulties occur and aiming neither to alter nor improve (nor even to reconcile us to them), are the most important points at which the problems of political philosophy become the general problems with which European philosophers have normally been concerned.

Political science—the taking thought to deal with each situation by hypothesis and experiment—is, in these conditions and in an academic setting, an impossibility. In an academic setting hypotheses are tools for the further elucidation of a subject-matter and they have no relevance to anything else. Political explanation exists here as philosophy and history, and nothing else. Political science, sociology, social administration, international relations, criminology, comparative institutions and comparative government, when looked at critically, dissolve into these two disciplines: and if they do not, they have not been looked at critically enough. The only political science, in this sense, goes on in the world of practice and the only political scientists are ministers and members of parliament, ambassadors and heads of department, kings, princes, citizens and revolutionaries who are, like historians, physicists and philosophers, responsible for the subject-matter on which they work. Professors of Political Science who want to engage in political practice (by standing for Parliament, writing in newspapers, advising governments or joining the City Council) are free to do so. But they are, so far as they do this, abandoning their academic function for a practical political one. To do so may, if they are lucky, help them to illuminate the academic subject-matter. But the only rational action to which scholars, as scholars, are committed, the only moral action to which they are commanded and the only 'social responsibility' to which their *professional* position compels them, is to use their energies in order to explain in its full diversity as much as they can of the nature of the world in which they live.

These pages have come to no very startling conclusion and will not, it is to be hoped, stimulate anyone to demonstrate in the streets, burn down Printing House Square or Broadcasting House, or feel any pressing duty to weigh his vote more carefully in the future. These are things which those who engage in political practice will look after and which the author as citizen will no doubt help to look after also. He does not question the usefulness of the language of principle as a convention in political practice, so long as political principles are seen to be arbitrary positions from which men do not propose to shift. But to justify action by reference to 'principle' is to describe the commitments which guide preferences in particular situations, not to postulate a pre-articulated universally right embodiment of principles formulated by philosophy. There are limits to the power of explanation, and one concern has been to suggest to those who want to increase understanding of the nature of political activity some of the lines on which they ought to do it.

Explanation is a form of action: and so is the making of books. And both, like political action, have their own conventions, rules and institutions. Character, temperament, industry and intelligence are demonstrable in both according to what men make of the situations with which they are confronted and the tools and talents they find to hand. Success in one, however, provides no guarantee of success elsewhere. To engage successfully in one involves diverting energy from the other. Just as in political practice little certainty need be attached to the intentions men promulgate and the actions they take, so, in political philosophy and explanation of the character of political activity, disappointment, discouragement, disillusionment and error will be avoided, not by making claims so large as to be unrealizable, but by observing the limits within which meaning, coherence and intelligibility are possible. This may not in the short run very obviously help in the maintenance of our lives, health and liberties and the avoidance of disaster to the society in which we live, but by this philosophers ought not to be disturbed. In political, as in all other activity, there are no guarantees—not even concern in a practical manner for the world as it is or unwillingness to pretend that it could be better than it can be. The function of philosophy is to assure itself that this is so and an important preoccupation of the philosopher should be to establish that his concern is no wider than it is.

Human society is the outcome of a series, extending over all generations, of acts of apparently arbitrary will which may be not less rational because they are the product of unargued and undefendable prejudice. Only a small part of the actions of each generation can be controlled by that particular generation and only the minutest fragment of what it inherits can be scrutinized to see whether it rises to a level suitable to human dignity. Each man, each group, each generation and each society nevertheless gives a push to human history: and some in doing so announce intentions. But whatever significance men in action attach to the intentions they announce, it is not just the intentions they announce which reveal the principles by which they are moved.

Moral action does not emerge from the utterance of irrelevant slogans—or even from the utterance of relevant ones—it emerges *ambulando*, in the full accomplishment of practice: and the more power a person has, the greater the opportunity for doing good. Political principles, political morality and the outcome of the practical political judgement are displayed through nothing less than the whole of human history and nothing less than the whole history of a group, generation or society is sufficient to reveal in full tension and fruitfulness what part of its moral and political obligations has been fulfilled. This emerges not just through writing, preaching and the enunciation of purposes: but through the energies of all its citizens moving forward in time, all attempting to reveal the full possibility of the activities to which they are committed and all between them playing a definite part in creating the world we know—a world of variety and invention the extent of whose success in fulfilling its possibilities cannot properly be known to any of its participants. All human activity reveals some part of the rationality implicit in human existence and it is only when the rationality of reflection is seen beside the manifestations apparent in the outcome of all other sorts of activity that reflection can do its work. There is rationality in existence but it is not disclosed by philosophy merely but in action also. It is to be found out: never completely found out, but found out to the extent to which men are capable of finding it. What a man thinks right bears some relation to what is right and the tension between the two is the history of his life. The world can judge success and conformity to the positive law but it can judge little else. Biography and some sorts of confessional and psychological explanation can begin to measure the complexity of the connection between opportunity and accomplishment but, even with the best of intentions and in the most sympathetic hands, neither can reveal much. The merit, character and nature of the reaction each man makes to his world is effected by him and in part known to him and then lost to all time. His character, merit and rationality, and the success he has in developing the possibilities that are open to him, can be grasped so imperfectly by others that the judgements of others are likely to be inadequate. The only substantial knowledge in these matters is self-knowledge and the only use of self-knowledge is, not as a guide to action and not to dispose of the moral characters of other men, but as confirmation of the fact that Mind, Being, Goodness and Energy are *everywhere* struggling to exist before us.

This, if it deserves consideration at all, may seem sceptical, reactionary and ontological: but not necessarily, and not in any case necessarily to disadvantage. If it makes nonsense in explanation of the practical pretension to judge political action by anything more than the passing prejudices a man happens to have, that is what it is intended to do. If it disposes of the pretensions of those who claim sympathy for all sorts of human experience, and yet (like Mill) have sympathy for only one, then good will have been done. And if recognition of the fact that rationality is implicit and moral quality present in differing degrees in *all* action extends one's sympathies beyond the rim of one's own experience to comprehend (and, where comprehension is impossible, blindly to salute) the efforts all men make with varying degrees of success with the talents, opportunities and temperaments they have to hand to realize the possibilities which historians reveal through history and philosophers through philosophy, a great deal will have been accomplished. For it is only by being concerned to discern, explain or blindly salute the goodness, rationality and Being which are, together with much else, disposed about *all* parts of the world of practice that political studies in general, and political philosophy in particular, are likely to achieve that consistent, explanatory sanity of which a necessary pedantic modesty on the one hand and the unnecessary illusion of practical grandeur on the other have for too long deprived them.